ROBERT N. ANTHONY
Harvard Business School

and

LESLIE K. BREITNER
University of Washington Evans School
of Public Affairs

Essentials of
Accounti⸺ ⸺eview

H EDITION

PEARSON
Prentice
Hall

Upper Saddle River, New Jersey 07458

Library of Congress Cataloging-in-Publication Data

Anthony, Robert Newton
   Essentials of accounting review / Robert N. Anthony, and Leslie K. Breitner. – 9th ed.
     P. cm.
   Rev. ed. of: Core concepts of accounting / Robert N. Anthony, Leslie K. Breitner.—
8th ed. c2003
    ISBN 0-13-149695-6
   1. Accounting. I. Breitner, Leslie Pearlman. II. Anthony, Robert Newton. –Core
concepts of accounting. III. Title.
    HF5635.A6878 2006
    657–dc22

                                   2005035392

Senior Acquisitions Editor: Wendy Craven
VP/Editorial Director: Jeff Shelstad
Manager, Product Development: Pamela Hersperger
Project Manager: Kerri Tomasso
Project Development Manager, Media: Nancy Welcher
Executive Marketing Manager: John Wannemacher
Managing Editor, Production: Cynthia Regan
Manufacturing Coordinator: Indira Gutierrez
Cover Design: Kiwi Design
Cover Illustration/Photo: Roberto Mettifogo/Photonica/Getty Images, Inc.
Composition, Full-Service Project Management: Carlisle Publishing Services
Printer/Binder: RR Donnelley-Harrisonburg
Typeface: Times

Pearson Education LTD.   Pearson Education Australia PTY, Limited
Pearson Education Singapore, Pte. Ltd   Pearson Education North Asia Ltd
Pearson Education, Canada, Ltd   Pearson Educación de Mexico, S.A. de C.V.
Pearson Educaton—Japan   Pearson Education. Upper Saddle River. New Jersey

10 9 8 7 6 5 4 3
ISBN 0-13-149695-6

How to Use This Book

This book is intended primarily for those who are studying, or who have completed, the programmed text *Essentials of Accounting,* 9th edition. It contains the complete text of every point made in that book.

You can use it either to review the meaning of an accounting term or to review an entire topic. Usually, the easiest way to review a term is to look it up in the Glossary. The Glossary gives a short explanation.

If you want to review a whole topic, you can refer to the Table of Contents for the part and section in which the topic is discussed.

If you have been introduced to accounting by another book, you can review terms or topics in the same way. However, this book, as is the case with all accounting texts, is not by itself a satisfactory way of learning the subject. Students need the "hands-on" experience that is provided by the programmed text or the computer.

Contents

Part 1
Basic Concepts   1

ELEMENTS OF THE BALANCE SHEET   3
ASSETS   3
LIABILITIES AND EQUITY   3
DUAL-ASPECT CONCEPT   4
MONEY-MEASUREMENT CONCEPT   5
ENTITY CONCEPT   6
GONG-CONCERN CONCEPT   7
ASSET-MANAGEMENT CONCEPT   8
BALANCE SHEET ITEMS   9
ASSETS   10
LIABILITIES   11
CURRENT RATIO   11
EQUITY   12
KEY POINTS TO REMEMBER 13

Part 2
Balance Sheet Changes; Income Measurement   15

CURRENT ASSETS   15
NONCURRENT ASSETS   16

CURRENT LIABILITIES   17
NONCURRENT LIABILITIES   18
EQUITY   18
BALANCE SHEET CHANGES   18
INCOME MEASUREMENT   26
KEY POINTS TO REMEMBER   29

Part 3
Accounting Records and Systems   31

THE ACCOUNT   31
RULES FOR INCREASES AND DECREASES   33
DEBIT AND CREDIT   35
INCOME STATEMENT ACCOUNTS   36
THE LEDGER AND THE JOURNAL   37
THE CLOSING PROCESS   38
A NOTE ON COMPUTERS   41
KEY POINTS TO REMEMBER   42

Part 4
Revenues and Monetary Assets   45

FISCAL YEAR   46
ACCRUAL ACCOUNTING   46
CONSERVATISM   47
MATERIALITY   48
REALIZATION   48
SERVICE REVENUE   51
AMOUNT OF REVENUE   52
MONETARY ASSETS   54
DAYS' SALES UNCOLLECTED   55
KEY POINTS TO REMEMBER   55

Part 5
Expense Measurement; The Income Statement   57

EXPENSE AND EXPENDITURE   58
UNEXPIRED AND EXPIRED COSTS   60
MATCHING CONCEPT   60
OTHER ASSETS THAT WILL BECOME EXPENSES   61
EXPENSES THAT CREATE LIABILITIES   62
FRINGE BENEFITS   63

RENT EXPENSE   64
LOSSES   64
SUMMARY OF MATCHING CONCEPT   65
AN EXAMPLE OF MATCHING   65
THE INCOME STATEMENT   69
A PACKAGE OF ACCOUNTING REPORTS   69
INCOME STATEMENT PERCENTAGES   71
REVIEW OF BASIC CONCEPTS   71
KEY POINTS TO REMEMBER   72

Part 6
Inventories and Cost of Sales   73

FINDING COST OF SALES   73
INVENTORY VALUATION: ASSUMPTIONS   77
FIRST-IN, FIRST-OUT (FIFO) METHOD   79
LAST-IN, FIRST-OUT (LIFO) METHOD   79
AVERAGE-COST METHOD   80
COMPARISON OF INVENTORY METHODS   80
INVENTORY VALUATION: ADJUSTMENT TO MARKET   81
INVENTORY IN A MANUFACTURING COMPANY   81
PRODUCT COSTS AND PERIOD COSTS   83
OVERHEAD RATES   83
INVENTORY TURNOVER   84
KEY POINTS TO REMEMBER   85

Part 7
Noncurrent Assets and Depreciation   87

NONCURRENT ASSETS   87
ACCOUNTING FOR ACQUISITIONS   88
CAPITAL LEASES   88
DEPRECIATION   89
DEPRECIATION METHODS   91
    Units-of-Production Depreciation   91
    Straight-Line Depreciation   92
    Accelerated Depreciation   93
ACCOUNTING FOR DEPRECIATION   94
    Sale of a Plant Asset   96
    Significance of Depreciation   96
DEPLETION   97
INTANGIBLE ASSETS   97
KEY POINTS TO REMEMBER   98

Part 8
Liabilities and Equity   101

WORKING CAPITAL   101
SOURCES OF CAPITAL   102
DEBT CAPITAL   103
TYPES OF EQUITY CAPITAL   104
   Common Stock   106
   Preferred Stock   107
RETAINED EARNINGS AND DIVIDENDS   108
DISTRIBUTIONS TO SHAREHOLDERS   108
BALANCE BETWEEN DEBT AND EQUITY CAPITAL   109
DEBT RATIO   111
CONSOLIDATED FINANCIAL STATEMENTS   112
KEY POINTS TO REMEMBER   114

Part 9
Statement of Cash Flows   117

CASH FLOW FROM OPERATING ACTIVITIES   120
ADJUSTMENTS FOR DEPRECIATION EXPENSE   121
ADJUSTMENTS FOR CHANGES IN WORKING
CAPITAL ACCOUNTS   122
ADJUSTMENTS FOR CHANGES IN CURRENT ASSETS   122
   No Change in Balance   122
   Current Asset Balance Decreased   123
   Current Asset Balance Increases   124
   Analysis with Diagrams   124
ADJUSTMENTS FOR CHANGES IN CURRENT LIABILITIES   127
NET EFFECT OF WORKING CAPITAL CHANGES   127
SUMMARY OF OPERATING ADJUSTMENTS   128
CASH FLOW FROM INVESTING AND FINANCING ACTIVITIES   129
   Investing Activities   129
   Financing Activities   129
COMPLETING THE STATEMENT OF CASH FLOWS   130
USES OF THE STATEMENT OF CASH FLOWS   131
KEY POINTS TO REMEMBER   131

Part 10
Analysis of Financial Statements   133

LIMITATIONS OF FINANCIAL STATEMENT ANALYSIS   133
AUDITING   134
OVERALL FINANCIAL MEASURES OF PERFORMANCE   134
FACTORS AFFECTING RETURN ON EQUITY   136

TESTS OF CAPITAL UTILIZATION   139
OTHER MEASURES OF PERFORMANCE   142
PROFITABILITY MEASUREMENT   144
TESTS OF FINANCIAL CONDITION   145
QUALITY OF EARNINGS   145
THE SARBANES-OXLEY ACT OF 2002   149
KEY POINTS TO REMEMBER   151

Part 11
Nonprofit Financial Statements   153

NONPROFIT ORGANIZATIONS   153
MISSIONS AND GOALS   155
NET ASSETS   155
REVENUES, EXPENSES, AND INVESTMENTS   156
TRANSFERS   160
SIMILARITIES TO FINANCIAL STATEMENTS
OF FOR-PROFIT ENTITIES   161
LIMITATION OF RATIO ANALYSIS   161
KEY POINTS TO REMEMBER   162

Part 12
Government Accounting   163

THE NATURE OF GOVERNMENT ACCOUNTING   163
LEVELS OF GOVERNMENT   165
ACCOUNTABILITY AND PERFORMANCE   166
FINANCIAL REPORTING-A MUNICIPALITY   169

CONCLUDING NOTE   177

ACKNOWLEDGMENTS   177

GLOSSARY   179

PART 1

Basic Concepts

This part describes
- The nature of the balance sheet
- The accounting meaning of assets, liabilities, and equity
- The first five of the nine concepts that govern all accounting:
  - The dual-aspect concept
  - The money-measurement concept
  - The entity concept
  - The going-concern concept
  - The asset-measurement concept
- The meaning of the principal items reported on a balance sheet

Accounting is a language. The purpose of any language is to convey information. Accounting information is provided by reports called **financial statements.** This book will help you understand what the numbers in the financial statements mean and how they can be used. Exhibit 1.1 shows one of these financial statements; this report is called a **balance sheet.**

Exhibit 1.1

GARSDEN COMPANY

Balance Sheet
as of December 31, 2006
($000 omitted)

ASSETS		LIABILITIES AND EQUITY	

CURRENT ASSETS

		CURRENT LIABILITIES	
Cash	$ 1,449	Accounts payable	$ 5,602
Marketable securities	246	Bank loan payable	1,000
Accounts receivable, net	9,944	Accrued liabilities	876
Inventories	10,623	Estimated tax liability	1,541
Prepaid expenses	389	Current portion of long-term debt	500
Total current assets	22,651	Total current liabilities	9,519

NONCURRENT ASSETS

		NONCURRENT LIABILITIES	
Property, plant, equipment at cost	$26,946	Long-term debt, less current portion	2,000
Accumulated depreciation	− 13,534	Deferred income taxes	824
Property, plant, equipment—net	13,412	Total liabilities	12,343
Investments	1,110		
Patents and trademarks	403		
Goodwill	663		
Total noncurrent assets	15,588		

EQUITY

		Common stock	1,000
		Additional paid-in capital	11,256
		Total paid-in capital	12,256
		Retained earnings	13,640
		Total equity	25,896
		TOTAL LIABILITIES	
TOTAL ASSETS	$38,239	& EQUITY	$38,239

ELEMENTS OF THE BALANCE SHEET

A balance sheet gives financial information about an **entity.** The entity that Exhibit 1.1 refers to is Garsden Company. An entity is any organization for which financial statements are prepared. A business is an entity; a college, a government, a church, and a synagogue are also entities.

The balance sheet is a snapshot of the financial position of the entity as of one moment in time. The balance sheet for Garsden Company reports its financial position as of December 31, 2006. This date is the date to which the report applies and not the date on which it was prepared. Thus, the heading tells three things:

1. The fact that the report is a balance sheet
2. The name of the entity
3. The date to which the report applies

The Garsden Company balance sheet has two sides: the left, Assets, and the right, Liabilities and Equity. We will describe the meaning of each side. In fact, the Assets section may appear above the Liabilities and Equity section in some financial statements.

ASSETS

Assets are valuable resources owned by the entity. An entity needs cash, equipment, and other resources in order to operate. These resources are its assets. The left side of the balance sheet shows the amount of each of these assets as of a certain date. For example, the amount of Cash that Garsden Company owned on December 31, 2006, was $1,449,000.

Assets are resources owned by Garsden Company. Its employees, although usually its most valuable resource, are not assets in accounting, because the company does not own its employees.

LIABILITIES AND EQUITY

The right side of the balance sheet shows the sources of funds that provided the entity's assets. As the heading indicates, there are two general types of sources, liabilities and equity.

Liabilities are obligations of the entity to outside parties who have furnished resources. These parties are generally called **creditors** because they have extended credit to the entity. As Exhibit 1.1 indicates, suppliers have extended credit in the amount of $5,602,000 as indicated by the item accounts payable.

Creditors have a **claim** against the assets in the amount shown as the liability. For example, a bank has loaned $1,000,000 to Garsden Company and therefore has a current claim of this amount, as indicated by the item Bank loan payable.

Because an entity will use its assets to pay its claims, the claims are claims against assets. They are claims against *all* the assets, not any particular asset.

The other source of the funds that an entity uses to acquire its assets is called **Equity.** The name is Equity (singular) not Equities (plural), even though there are several sources of equity. There are two sources of equity funds: (1) the amount provided directly by equity investors, which is called **Total paid-in capital,** and (2) the amount retained from profits (or earnings)—that is, the amount of earnings that has not been paid to equity investors in the form of dividends—which is called **Retained earnings.**

Creditors can sue the entity if the amounts due them are not paid. Equity investors have only a residual claim; if the entity is dissolved, they get whatever is left after the liabilities have been paid, which may be nothing. Liabilities therefore are a stronger claim against the assets than equity.

We can describe the right-hand side of the balance sheet in two somewhat different ways: (1) as the amount of funds supplied by creditors and equity investors and (2) as the claims of these parties against the assets. Both are correct.

DUAL-ASPECT CONCEPT

The assets that remain after the liabilities are taken into account will be claimed by the equity investors. If an entity has assets that total $10,000, and liabilities that total $4,000, its equity must be $6,000.

Because (1) any assets not claimed by creditors will be claimed by equity investors and (2) the total amount of claims (liabilities + equity) cannot exceed what there is to be claimed, it follows that the total amount of assets will always be equal to the total amount of liabilities plus equity.

The fact that total assets must equal, or **balance,** total liabilities plus equity is why the statement is called a balance sheet. This equality tells nothing about the entity's financial condition; it always exists unless the accountant has made a mistake.

This fact leads to what is called the **dual-aspect concept.** The two aspects to which this concept refers are (1) assets and (2) liabilities plus equity, and the concept states that these two aspects are always equal. (This equality exists even if liabilities are greater than assets. For example, if assets in an unprofitable business were $100,000 and liabilities were $120,000, equity would be a negative amount of $20,000.)

The dual-aspect concept is the first of nine fundamental accounting concepts we shall describe in this book. The concept can be written as an equation:

$$\textbf{Assets} = \textbf{Liabilities} + \textbf{Equity}$$

This equation is fundamental. It governs all accounting. We can write a similar equation in a form that emphasizes the fact that equity is a residual interest:

$$\textbf{Assets} - \textbf{Liabilities} = \textbf{Equity}$$

For example, if the assets of Otis Company total $20,000 and its liabilities total $18,000, its equity must total $2,000.

Always equal!

The two sides **balance.**

The term "Net assets" is sometimes used instead of "equity." It refers to the fact that Equity is always the difference between Assets and Liabilities.

MONEY-MEASUREMENT CONCEPT

If a fruit store owned $200 in cash, 100 dozen oranges, and 200 apples, you could not add up its total assets from this information, because you can't add apples and oranges. But if you knew that the 100 dozen oranges cost

$5 a dozen and the 200 apples cost $0.40 each, you could then add these amounts to the $200 cash and find the total assets to be $780 [= (100 × $5) + (200 × $0.40) + $200].

Thus, to be addable, amounts of different kinds of objects must be stated in similar units. The unit that appears in an accounting report is money—that is, dollars and cents. This is the **money-measurement concept.** By converting different facts to monetary amounts, we can deal with them arithmetically; that is, we can add one item to another, or we can subtract one item from another.

The money-measurement concept states that accounting reports only those facts that can be stated as monetary amounts. For example, the following facts could not be learned by reading a balance sheet of Able Company:

- The health of the president of Able Company
- Whether a strike is beginning at Able Company
- How many automobiles Able Company owns (the number of automobiles owned is not a monetary amount)

Because accounting reports include only facts that can be stated in monetary amounts, accounting is necessarily an incomplete record of the status of a business and does not always give the most important facts about it.

ENTITY CONCEPT

Accounts are kept for **entities,** rather than for the persons who own, operate, or otherwise are associated with those entities. For example, suppose Green Company is a business entity and Sue Smith is its owner. Sue Smith withdraws $100 from the business. In preparing financial accounts for Green Company, we should record the effect of this withdrawal on the accounts of the entity.

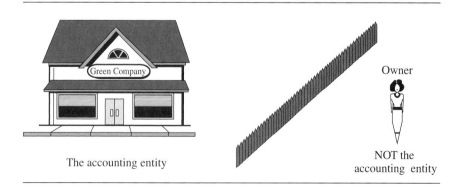

The accounting entity

Owner

NOT the accounting entity

If Sue Smith withdraws $100 from Green Company, of which she is the sole owner, Smith now has $100 more cash, but she has $100 less equity in Green Company. Smith is, therefore, no better or worse than she was before. What about Green Company? It now has $100 less in assets. Thus, an event can affect the owner in one way and the entity in another way. Financial statements of Green Company report only the effect that events have on the entity. (Of course, Sue Smith can have her own personal financial statements.)

The fact that accounts are kept for entities as distinguished from the persons associated with those entities is called the **entity concept.**

Owners of some small retail stores (called "mom and pop" stores) may not identify the cost of merchandise they withdraw for personal use, personal telephone calls, and the like. If this is so, then they do not apply the entity concept. Consequently, the financial statements of these stores are inaccurate.

A business may be organized under any one of several legal forms: a corporation, a partnership (two or more owners), or a proprietorship (a single owner). The entity concept applies, regardless of the legal status. Municipalities, hospitals, religious organizations, colleges, and other nonbusiness organizations are also accounting entities. Although in this book we focus on businesses, the accounting for nonbusiness entities is similar.

GOING-CONCERN CONCEPT

Every year, some entities go bankrupt or cease to operate for other reasons. Most entities, however, keep on going from one year to the next. Accounting must assume either that (1) entities are about to cease operations or (2) they are likely to keep on going. In general, the more realistic assumption is that an entity, or **concern,** normally will keep on *going* from one year to the next. This assumption is called the **going-concern concept.**

Specifically, the going-concern concept states that accounting assumes that an entity will continue to operate indefinitely unless there is evidence to the contrary. (If the entity is not a going concern, special accounting rules apply; they are not discussed in this introductory book.)

Because of the going-concern concept, accounting does not report what the assets could be sold for if the entity ceased to exist. On December 31, 2005, the balance sheet of Evans Company reported total assets of $500,000. If Evans Company ceased to operate, we do not know what its assets could be sold for.

We next describe the concepts that govern the measurement of asset amounts on the balance sheet. Most monetary assets are reported at their *fair value,* and most nonmonetary assets are reported at an amount that is based on their *cost.* These concepts, and the reasoning behind them, are introduced in that section.

ASSET-MEASUREMENT CONCEPT

When an entity buys an asset, it records the amount of the asset at its cost. Thus, if Georgia Company bought a plot of land for $10,000 in 2005, it would report on its December 31, 2005, balance sheet the item: land, $10,000.

Readers of the balance sheet want to know what the reported assets are worth. In accounting, the name for what an asset is "worth" is its **fair value** (also called market value). The Garsden Company balance sheet (Exhibit 1.1) reported that the company's cash on December 31, 2006, was $1,449,000. This was the fair value of the asset cash. We can be reasonably certain that the amount was actually $1,449,000 because the banks in which cash was deposited have reliable records of this amount.

Also, we can be reasonably certain that the fair value of marketable securities was $246,000 because a stock exchange publishes a reliable record of the value as of December 31, 2006, for each security that it trades. In general, an asset is reported at its fair value when reliable information as to its market value is available. Usually, this information is obtained from an outside party. The **asset-measurement concept** states that, if reliable information is available, an asset is measured at its cost.

The fair value of most assets is known on the date the asset was acquired because the buyer and the seller agreed on the amount. If Garsden Company purchased a plot of land in 1996 for $100,000, this land would have been reported on its December 31, 1996, balance sheet as $100,000. Because Garsden Company does not know the fair value of the land on December 31, 2006, Garsden would report the amount at $100,000, which was its cost.

If on December 31, 2006, Garsden owned machinery that it had purchased 5 years earlier for $50,000 with an estimated life of 10 years, it would probably report the asset amount at less than $50,000, representing the amount of cost that has not yet been used up. (Calculating this amount involves depreciation, described later in this book.)

In general, land, buildings, equipment, and inventories have this characteristic; their fair value cannot be measured reliably except at the time they are acquired. Thus, they are reported at cost or a number based on cost.

The asset-measurement concept combines both types of assets illustrated in this section. If reliable information is available, the amount of an asset is measured at its fair value. Otherwise, the measurement is based on its cost.

There are two reasons for measuring some assets at cost. First, estimating fair value of each asset may be expensive and unreliable. If you bought a pair of shoes for $100 in 2005 and asked two friends in 2006 for the shoes' value, they probably would disagree. Even if the estimates were made by professionals, the appraised value of each asset in a company would be subjective. Second, many assets are not going to be sold in the near future; they will be used in ongoing operations. The entity and those who use its balance sheet therefore do not need to know the fair value of these assets. This reason stems from the going-concern concept.

To summarize, the two reasons that accounting focuses on costs rather than on fair values for some assets are

- Fair values are difficult to estimate; that is, they are subjective, whereas costs are objective.

- The going-concern concept makes it unnecessary to know the market value of many assets; the assets will be used in future operations rather than being sold immediately.

The decision as to whether an asset is accounted for at fair value or at cost is usually made at the time the asset is acquired. For example, if a shoe retailer purchased an inventory of shoes for $1,000, they would be accounted for $1,000, which was their cost. If the retailer expected to sell the shoes for at least $1,500, they would be reported on the balance sheet at $1,000, their cost.

Monetary assets are those that have a claim on a specified amount of money. Cash, securities, and bonds are monetary assets. Land, buildings, equipment, and inventory are nonmonetary assets. In general—but with some exceptions, described in later parts—monetary assets are reported at fair value; nonmonetary assets are reported at cost or an amount based on cost.

Accounting does not report what many of the individual assets are worth—that is, their fair value. Accounting therefore does not report what the whole entity is worth. Those who criticize accounting for its failure to report an entity's "worth" do not appreciate that to do so would be difficult, subjective, and unnecessary.

BALANCE SHEET ITEMS

Refer back to Exhibit 1.1, which reports the amounts of assets, liabilities, and equity of Garsden Company as of December 31, 2006. The note "($000 omitted)" means that the numbers are reported in thousands of dollars. For example, the number reported for cash, $1,449, means that the amount of cash was $1,449,000. This is common practice. It is done to make the numbers easier to read; users are not interested in the details of the last three digits.

The total of the assets always equals the total of the liabilities plus equity. Total assets were $38,239,000, and total liabilities plus equity were $38,239,000. Most items on a balance sheet are summaries of more detailed accounts. For example, the cash is probably located in a number of separate bank accounts, in cash registers, and in petty cash boxes. The total of all the cash is $1,449,000, rounded to the nearest thousand dollars.

ASSETS

Earlier, we referred to assets as valuable resources, or things of value. Let's make this idea more specific. In order to count as an asset in accounting, an item must meet three requirements.

The first requirement is that the item must be *controlled* by the entity. Usually, this means that the entity must *own* the item. If Able Company rents a building owned by Baker Company, this building is not an asset of Able Company. The building is an asset of Baker Company. Certain leases, called capital leases, are assets and are an exception to this rule. They are described in Part 7.

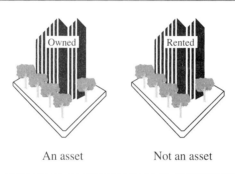

An asset   Not an asset

In accounting, the employees of an entity are not assets because the entity does not own them. However, if a baseball club owns a contract in which a player agrees to provide services, the contract is an asset.

The second requirement is that the item must be *valuable* to the entity. Because of this requirement, the following items do not qualify as assets of a company that sells dresses, even though they are owned:

- Dresses that no one wants because they have gone out of style

- A cash register that doesn't work and can't be repaired

The third requirement is that the item must have been acquired at a *measurable cost.* Jones Company bought a trademark from another company for $1 million; this trademark is an asset of Jones Company. By contrast, if Jones Company has built up an excellent reputation because of the consistently high quality of its products, this reputation is not an asset in accounting, even though it may be worth many millions of dollars.

To summarize, for an item to be listed as an asset, it must meet three requirements:

1. It must be owned or controlled by the entity.
2. It must be valuable to the entity.
3. It must have been acquired at a measurable cost.

Assets are divided into two main categories—current and noncurrent—and liabilities are divided into these categories. They are introduced in the following section and explained in more detail in Part 2.

Current assets are cash and other assets that are expected to be converted into cash or used up in the near future, usually within one year. Groceries on the shelves of a grocery store are current assets. The store building is not a current asset. On the balance sheet, current assets are usually reported separately from noncurrent assets. They are expected to be converted to cash within a year.

Current assets consist of cash and of assets that are expected to be converted into cash or used up within a short period, usually within one year. As the name suggests, assets that are expected to be useful for longer than one future year are called noncurrent assets.

LIABILITIES

The right-hand side of the Garsden Company balance sheet lists the company's liabilities and equity. These can be regarded either as **claims** against the assets or as the **sources** from which the assets were acquired. The claims of creditors and other outside parties are called **liabilities.**

In Exhibit 1.1, the first category of liabilities is **current liabilities.** As you might expect from the discussion of current assets, current liabilities are claims that become due within a short time, usually within one year. Garsden Company has obtained funds by borrowing, and $2,000,000 of this debt is not due to be repaid until after December 31, 2007. This amount is therefore a noncurrent liability.

Liabilities are claims against *all* the assets. The $5,602,000 of **accounts payable** on the Garsden Company balance sheet is a claim against the total assets of $38,239,000.

CURRENT RATIO

The **current assets** and **current liabilities** indicate the entity's ability to meet its current obligations. A measure of this ability is the current ratio, which is the ratio of current assets to current liabilities. For Garsden

Company, the current ratio is 2.4 to 1 [$22,651,000/$9,519,000]. If, in Garsden's industry, a current ratio of at least 2 to 1 is desirable, then Garsden Company passes this test.

EQUITY

Equity consists of capital obtained from sources that are not liabilities. As Exhibit 1.1 indicates, there are two sources of equity capital:

- $12,256,000, which is labeled total paid-in capital
- $13,640,000, which is labeled retained earnings

Paid-in Capital is the amount of capital supplied by equity investors. They own the entity. The detail of how this item is reported depends on the type of organization. Garsden Company is a corporation, and its owners receive shares of **common stock** as evidence of their ownership. They are therefore called **shareholders (or stockholders).** Other forms of ownership will be described in Part 8.

The Paid-in Capital is reported as two separate amounts: $1,000,000, which is labeled Common Stock, and $11,256,000, labeled Additional Paid-in Capital. The reasons for this distinction are described in Part 8. The important number is the total amount paid in by the shareholders, which is $12,256,000.

Individual shareholders may sell their stock to someone else, but this has no effect on the balance sheet of the corporation. The market price of shares of General Motors Corporation stock changes practically every day; the amount of Paid-in Capital reported on the General Motors balance sheet does not reflect these changes. This is consistent with the entity concept; transactions between individual shareholders do not affect the entity.

The other equity item, $13,640,000, shows the amount of equity that has been earned by the profitable operations of the company and that has been retained in the entity, hence the name **Retained Earnings.** Retained Earnings represents those amounts that have been retained in the entity after parts of the company's earnings (i.e., profits) have been paid to shareholders in the form of dividends.

Retained Earnings are additions to equity that have accumulated since the entity began, not those of a single year. Therefore, unless Garsden Company has been in business only one year, the $13,640,000 shown as Retained Earnings as of December 31, 2006, reflects all previous years of operations.

The amount of Retained Earnings shows the amount of capital generated by operating activities. It is not cash. Cash is an asset. On December 31, 2006, the amount of Cash was $1,449,000. The amount of Retained Earnings was $13,640,000.

Always keep in mind the fundamental accounting equation:

$$\textbf{Assets} = \textbf{Liabilities} + \textbf{Equity}$$

The right-hand side of the balance sheet shows the sources of capital. The capital itself exists in the form of assets, which are reported on the left-hand side.

KEY POINTS TO REMEMBER

- The assets of an entity are the things of value that it owns.

- The sources of funds used to acquire assets are (1) liabilities and (2) equity.

- Liabilities are sources from creditors.

- Equity consists of (1) funds obtained from equity investors, who are owners, and (2) retained earnings, which result from the entity's profitable operation.

- Creditors have a strong claim on the assets. They can sue if the amounts due them are not paid. Equity investors have only a residual claim.

- Total assets equal the total of liabilities plus equity. This is the dual-aspect concept.

- The amounts of assets, liabilities, and equity as of one point in time are reported on the entity's balance sheet.

- Accounting reports only those facts that can be stated in monetary amounts. This is the money-measurement concept.

- Business accounts are kept for entities, rather than for the persons who own, operate, or otherwise are associated with those entities. This is the entity concept.

- Accounting assumes that an entity will continue to operate indefinitely. This is the going-concern concept.

- Monetary assets are reported at their fair value; other assets are reported at a number based on cost. This is the asset-measurement concept.

- Assets are valuable items that are owned or controlled by the entity and that were acquired at a measurable cost. Goodwill is not an asset unless it was purchased.

- Current assets are cash and other assets that are expected to be converted into cash or used up in the near future, usually within one year.

- Current liabilities are obligations due in the near future, usually within one year.

- The current ratio is the ratio of current assets to current liabilities.

- Equity consists of paid-in capital (which in a corporation is represented by shares of stock) plus earnings retained since the entity began. It does not report the market value of the stock. Retained Earnings is not cash; it is part of the owners' claim on the assets.

PART 2

Balance Sheet Changes; Income Measurement

This part describes
- The meaning of the principal items reported on a balance sheet
- How several types of transactions change the amounts reported on the balance sheet
- The nature of income and the income statement

CURRENT ASSETS

Assets are divided into two main categories, as indicated in Part 1: current and noncurrent. Liabilities are also divided into these categories. They are explained in more detail in the following sections.

Current assets are cash and other assets that are expected to be converted into cash or used up in the near future, usually within one year.

Securities are stocks and bonds. They give valuable rights to the entity that owns them. The U.S. Treasury promises to pay stated amounts of money to entities that own treasury bonds. Therefore, U.S. Treasury Bonds owned by an entity are assets of that entity. **Marketable securities** are securities that are expected to be converted into cash within a year. An entity owns these securities so as to earn a return on funds that otherwise would be idle. Marketable securities are current assets. Investments in safe, very short-term funds, such as money market funds, are often included in the cash item rather than in marketable securities. The item is then called cash and cash equivalents.

An **account receivable** is an amount that is owed to the business, usually by one of its customers, as a result of the ordinary extension of credit. A customer's monthly bill from the electric company would be an account receivable of the electric company until the customer paid the bill.

Inventories are goods being held for sale, as well as supplies, raw materials, and partially finished products that will be sold upon completion. For example, a truck owned by an automobile dealer for resale to its customers is inventory. A truck owned by an entity and used to transport its own goods is not inventory. In Exhibit 1.1, the inventories of Garsden Company are reported as $10,623,000.

An entity's burglar alarm system is valuable because it provides protection against loss. The burglar alarm system is an asset. A fire insurance policy that protects the entity against losses caused by fire damage is also an asset. It has value to the entity. Entities buy fire insurance protection ahead of the period that the insurance policy covers. When they buy the insurance policy, they acquire an asset. Because the policy covers only a short period of time, the asset is a current asset. Insurance protection can't be touched. It is an **intangible** asset.

Prepaid Expenses is the name for intangible assets that will be used up in the near future; that is, they are intangible current assets. (The reason for using the word "expense" will be explained in Part 5.) Exhibit 1.1 shows that Garsden Company had $389,000 of Prepaid Expenses on December 31, 2006.

NONCURRENT ASSETS

Tangible assets are assets that can be touched; they have physical substance. Buildings, trucks, and machines are tangible assets. They are also **noncurrent assets.** As indicated by the first item listed under Noncurrent Assets in Exhibit 1.1, the usual name for tangible, noncurrent assets is Property, Plant, and Equipment. Because they are noncurrent, we know that these assets are expected to be used in the entity for more than one year.

Refer back to Exhibit 1.1, which shows the cost of property, plant, and equipment to be $26,946,000. It shows that a portion of the cost of this asset has been subtracted from the original cost because it has been "used up." This "used-up" portion is called **Accumulated Depreciation** and totals $13,534,000. After this amount is subtracted, the asset amount is shown as $13,412,000. This is the amount of cost that has not been used up. (In Part 7, we shall explain this amount further.)

The other noncurrent asset items are intangible assets; that is, they have no physical substance, except as pieces of paper. The **Investments** item consists of securities, such as bonds. Evidently, Garsden Company does not intend to turn these investments into cash within one year. If these securities were expected to be turned into cash within that period, they would be listed as a current asset, Marketable Securities.

The next noncurrent asset reported is **Patents and Trademarks.** These are rights to use patents and rights to valuable brand names or logos (such as "Advil"). Because they are assets, we know that

- They are valuable.

- They are owned by Garsden Company.

- They were acquired at a measurable cost.

Goodwill, the final item on the asset side, has a special meaning in accounting. It arises when one company buys another company and pays more than the value of its net identifiable assets. Grady Company bought Baker Company, paying $1,400,000 cash. Baker Company's identifiable assets were judged to be worth $1,500,000, and Grady became responsible for Baker's liabilities, which totaled $500,000. Therefore, goodwill was $400,000 [$1,400,000 – ($1,500,000 – $500,000)].

CURRENT LIABILITIES

As you might expect from the discussion of current assets, **current liabilities** are claims that become due within a short time, usually within one year. The first current liability listed in Exhibit 1.1 is **Accounts Payable.** These are the opposite of Accounts Receivable; that is, they are amounts that the company owes to its suppliers.

For example, in December 2005, Smith Company sold a personal computer to Brown Company for $3,000. Brown Company agreed to pay for it within 60 days. On its December 31, 2005, balance sheets, Smith Company would report the $3,000 as Accounts Receivable, and Brown Company would report the $3,000 as Accounts Payable.

The item **Bank Loan Payable** is reported separately from Accounts Payable because the debt is evidenced by a promissory note. In Exhibit 1.1, Garsden owes the bank $1,000,000. Amounts owed to employees and others for services they have provided but for which they have not been paid are listed as **Accrued Liabilities.** They will be described in Part 5.

Estimated Tax Liability is the amount owed to the government for taxes. It is shown separately from other liabilities, both because the amount is large and because the exact amount owed may not be known as of the date of the balance sheet. In Exhibit 1.1, this amount is shown as $1,541,000. It is a current liability because the amount is due within one year.

In the exhibit, two items of Long-Term Debt are shown as liabilities. One, labeled "current portion," amounts to $500,000. The other, listed under noncurrent liabilities, amounts to $2,000,000. Evidently, the total amount of long-term debt is $2,500,000.

The $500,000 is shown separately as a current liability because it is due within one year—that is, before December 31, 2007. The remaining $2,000,000 does not become due until after December 31, 2007.

NONCURRENT LIABILITIES

Suppose the $500,000 current portion was paid in 2007 and an additional $600,000 of debt became due in 2008. On the balance sheet as of December 31, 2007, the current portion of long-term debt would be reported as $600,000, and the noncurrent liability would be reduced to $1,400,000.

Although a single **liability** may have both a current portion and a noncurrent portion, a single asset is not always so divided. Prepaid Insurance of $2,000, covering protection for two future years, is usually reported as a current asset of $2,000.

EQUITY

Recall that **Equity** consists of capital obtained from sources that are not liabilities. The two sources of equity capital for Garsden Company are Total Paid-in Capital and Retained Earnings. Recall also that the amount of equity that has been *earned* by the profitable operations of the company and that has been *retained* in the entity is called Retained Earnings.

BALANCE SHEET CHANGES

The amounts of assets, liabilities, and equity of an entity change from day to day. Therefore, the amounts shown on its balance sheet also change. In this part, we will prepare a balance sheet at the end of each day. We will consider a business named Glendale Market, owned by a proprietor, John Smith.

On January 2, Smith started Glendale Market by opening a bank account in its name and depositing $10,000 of his money in it. Its balance sheet of January 2 appeared as follows:

GLENDALE MARKET

Balance Sheet as of January 2

Assets		Liabilities and Equity	
Cash	$10,000	Paid-in capital	$10,000
Total	$10,000	Total	$10,000

This balance sheet tells us how much cash Glendale Market had on January 2. The separation of Glendale Market from John Smith, the person, is an illustration of the entity concept. On January 2, Glendale Market received $10,000 cash from John Smith. To record the effect of this event on the financial condition of the entity, we made two changes in the balance sheet. After we made these changes, the balance sheet balanced. This is an illustration of the dual-aspect concept. A total should always be given for each side of the balance sheet.

An entity owned by one person, such as Glendale Market, is called a **proprietorship.** In some proprietorships, the equity item is labeled with the proprietor's name: "John Smith, Capital." This is simply a variation in terminology, not a difference in concepts.

When an entity borrows money, it may sign a written promise to repay. Such a written promise is termed a **note.** For example, if Business A borrows money from Business B, signing a note, Business A will record a note payable on its balance sheet, and Business B will record a note receivable.

On January 3, Glendale Market borrowed $5,000 cash from a bank, giving a note. Its balance sheet as of January 3 was as follows (items that were changed are shown in **boldface**):

GLENDALE MARKET

Balance Sheet as of January 3

Assets		Liabilities and Equity	
Cash	**$15,000**	**Note payable**	**$5,000**
		Paid-in capital	10,000
Total	**$15,000**	Total	**$15,000**

To record the effect of the event of January 3, two changes in the balance sheet (not counting the new totals and the new date) were necessary. The changes did not affect the equality that had existed between assets and liabilities + equity.

On January 4, Glendale Market purchased and received inventory costing $2,000, paying cash. Its balance sheet as of January 4 was as follows:

GLENDALE MARKET

Balance Sheet as of January 4

Assets		Liabilities and Equity	
Cash	**$13,000**	Note payable	$ 5,000
Inventory	**2,000**	Paid-in capital	10,000
Total	$15,000	Total	$15,000

The event of January 4 required two changes on the balance sheet, even though only one side of the balance sheet was affected.

Each event that is recorded in the accounting records is called a **transaction.** Each transaction causes at least two changes on the balance sheet (not counting the changes in totals and in the date), even when only one side of the balance sheet is affected. This is true of all transactions, and this is why accounting is called a **double-entry system.**

Earlier, we described the fundamental accounting equation, Assets = Liabilities + Equity. If we were to record only *one* aspect of a transaction, this equation would not continue to describe an equality. The fundamental accounting equation was also referred to in Part 1 as the dual-aspect concept.

When a business sells merchandise for $300 that had cost it $200, the profit of $100 represents an increase of $100 in equity. On January 5, Glendale Market sold merchandise for $300, receiving cash. The merchandise had cost $200. Its balance sheet as of January 5 was as follows:

GLENDALE MARKET

Balance Sheet as of January 5

Assets		Liabilities and Equity	
Cash	**$13,300**	Note payable	$ 5,000
Inventory	**1,800**	Paid-in capital	10,000
		Retained earnings	**100**
Total	**$15,100**	Total	**$15,100**

We can analyze the individual parts of this transaction as follows: Glendale Market sold merchandise for $300 cash that cost $200. Merchandise that had cost $200 was removed from its inventory. The transaction caused a net increase of $100 in the assets of Glendale Market from what they had been at the close of business on January 4. This increase was the result of selling the merchandise at a profit.

$15,100   = $15,100

On January 6, Glendale Market purchased merchandise for $2,000 and added it to its inventory. It agreed to pay the vendor within 30 days. An obligation to pay a vendor is called an Account Payable. Glendale Market's balance sheet as of January 6 was as follows:

GLENDALE MARKET

Balance Sheet as of January **6**

Assets		Liabilities and Equity	
Cash	$13,300	**Accounts payable**	**$ 2,000**
Inventory	**3,800**	Note payable	5,000
		Paid-in capital	10,000
		Retained earnings	100
Total	**$17,100**	Total	**$17,100**

On January 7, merchandise costing $500 was sold for $800, which was received in cash. The balance sheet as of January 7 was as follows:

GLENDALE MARKET

Balance Sheet as of January 7

Assets		Liabilities and Equity	
Cash	$14,100	Accounts payable	$ 2,000
Inventory	3,300	Note payable	5,000
		Paid-in capital	10,000
		Retained earnings	400
Total	$17,400	Total	$17,400

On January 8, merchandise costing $600 was sold for $900. The customer agreed to pay $900 within 30 days. When customers buy on credit, the entity has an asset called Accounts Receivable. The balance sheet as of January 8 was as follows:

GLENDALE MARKET

Balance Sheet as of January 8

Assets		Liabilities and Equity	
Cash	$14,100	Accounts payable	$ 2,000
Accounts receivable	**900**	Note payable	5,000
Inventory	2,700	Paid-in capital	10,000
		Retained earnings	700
Total	$17,700	Total	$17,700

On January 9, Glendale Market purchased a one-year insurance policy for $200, paying cash. Recall that the right to insurance protection is an asset. For this asset, use the term "Prepaid Insurance." The balance sheet as of January 9 was as follows:

GLENDALE MARKET

Balance Sheet as of January 9

Assets		Liabilities and Equity	
Cash	**$13,900**	Accounts payable	$ 2,000
Accounts receivable..................	900	Note payable............................	5,000
Inventory..................................	2,700	Paid-in capital..........................	10,000
Prepaid insurance..................	**200**	Retained earnings	700
Total	$17,700	Total	$17,700

On January 10, Glendale Market purchased two lots of land of equal size, for a total of $10,000. It thereby acquired an asset, Land. It paid $2,000 in cash and gave a 10-year mortgage for the balance of $8,000. Its balance sheet as of January 10 was as follows:

GLENDALE MARKET

Balance Sheet as of January 10

Assets		Liabilities and Equity	
Cash	**$11,900**	Accounts payable	$ 2,000
Accounts receivable..................	900	Note payable............................	5,000
Inventory..................................	2,700	**Mortgage payable**..................	**8,000**
Prepaid insurance	200	Paid-in capital..........................	10,000
Land..	**10,000**	Retained earnings	700
Total	**$25,700**	Total	**$25,700**

On January 11, Glendale Market sold one of the two lots of land for $5,000. The buyer paid $1,000 cash and assumed $4,000 of the mortgage; that is, Glendale Market was no longer responsible for this half of the mortgage payable. Its balance sheet as of January 11 was as follows:

GLENDALE MARKET

Balance Sheet as of January 11

Assets		Liabilities and Equity	
Cash	$12,900	Accounts payable	$ 2,000
Accounts receivable	900	Note payable	5,000
Inventory	2,700	Mortgage payable	4,000
Prepaid insurance	200	Paid-in capital	10,000
Land	5,000	Retained earnings	700
Total	$21,700	Total	$21,700

On January 12, Smith received an offer of $15,000 for his equity in Glendale Market. Although his equity was then only $10,700 (Paid-in Capital of $10,000 plus Retained Earnings of $700), he rejected the offer. It was evident that the store had already acquired goodwill with a market value of $4,300. This offer had no effect on the balance sheet. Goodwill is an asset only when it has been purchased. There was no transaction associated with this offer. Remember that the balance sheet does not show the fair value of the entity.

On January 13, Smith withdrew for his personal use $200 cash from the Glendale Market bank account, and he withdrew merchandise costing $400. Glendale Market's balance sheet as of January 13 was as follows:

GLENDALE MARKET

Balance Sheet as of January 13

Assets		Liabilities and Equity	
Cash	$12,700	Accounts payable	$ 2,000
Accounts receivable	900	Note payable	5,000
Inventory	2,300	Mortgage payable	4,000
Prepaid insurance	200	Paid-in capital	10,000
Land	5,000	Retained earnings	100
Total	$21,100	Total	$21,100

On January 14, Smith learned that the person who purchased the land on January 11 for $5,000 sold it for $8,000. The lot still owned by Glendale Market was identical in value to this other plot.

There is no effect on the balance sheet. Although the land still owned by Glendale Market may also have a fair value of $8,000, accounting does not consider fair values. There has been no **transaction** involving the Glendale Market land. That land continues to be reported at its cost of $5,000.

On January 15, Glendale Market paid off $2,000 of its bank loan, giving cash (disregard interest). Its balance sheet as of January 15 was as follows:

GLENDALE MARKET

Balance Sheet as of January 15

Assets		Liabilities and Equity	
Cash	$10,700	Accounts payable	$ 2,000
Accounts receivable	900	Note payable	3,000
Inventory	2,300	Mortgage payable	4,000
Prepaid insurance	200	Paid-in capital	10,000
Land	5,000	Retained earnings	100
Total	$19,100	Total	$19,100

On January 16, Glendale Market was changed to a corporation. John Smith received 100 shares of common stock in exchange for his $10,100 equity in the business. He immediately sold 25 of these shares for $4,000 cash.

John Smith's sale of shares has no effect on Glendale Market's balance sheet. Although there is a transaction here, it is a transaction between John Smith and the person who bought his shares. Glendale Market was not involved. (The name of the entity may have been changed to, say, Glendale Market Corporation, but this does not affect the numbers on the balance sheet.)

Any conceivable transaction can be recorded in terms of its effect on the balance sheet, just as we have done in this section. Although we shall describe techniques, refinements, and shortcuts in later parts, none of them changes this basic fact.

INCOME MEASUREMENT

As explained in Part 1, an entity's equity increases for either of two reasons. One is the receipt of capital from owners. On January 2, Glendale Market received $10,000 from John Smith, its owner. We recorded this as an increase in Cash and an increase in the equity item, Paid-in Capital.

The other source of an increase in equity is the **profitable operation** of the entity. Transactions that increase profit also increase the equity item, Retained Earnings. In the following table, we show the dollar amount of the change in Retained Earnings, if any, that resulted from each transaction from January 3 through 8.

Date	Nature	Retained Earnings	
		Increased by	No effect
3	Borrowing		X
4	Purchase		X
5	Sale	$100	
6	Purchase		X
7	Sale	300	
8	Sale	300	
	Total	$700	

As can be seen from the table, three of these transactions did not affect Retained Earnings: borrowing money and purchasing merchandise. The sale of that merchandise, however, did affect Retained Earnings.

The amount by which equity increased as a result of operations during a period of time is called the **income** of that period. We have just calculated that the total increase during the period January 2 through 8 was 700, so Glendale Market's income for that period was $700.

The amount of income and how it was earned is usually the most important financial information about a business entity. An accounting report called the **income statement** explains the income of a period. Note that the income statement is for a period of time, in contrast with the other statement, the balance sheet, which is for a point in time. The income statement explains *why* an increase occurred.

To understand how the income statement does this, let's look at the January 5 transaction for Glendale Market. On January 5, Glendale Market sold for $300 cash some merchandise that had cost $200. This caused equity (Retained Earnings) to increase/decrease by $100. This transaction consists of two separate events: (1) the sale, which, by itself, increased Retained Earnings by $300 and (2) the decrease in inventory, which, by itself, decreased Retained Earnings by $200.

By itself, the increase in Retained Earnings resulting from operations is called revenue. When Glendale Market sold merchandise for $300, the transaction resulted in $300 of revenue. By itself, the associated decrease in Retained Earnings is called an **expense.** When Glendale Market transferred merchandise to the customer, the transaction reduced inventory and resulted in $200 of expense.

Thus, when Glendale Market sold merchandise for $300 that cost $200, the effect of the transaction on Retained Earnings can be separated into two parts: a revenue of $300 and an expense of $200.

In accounting, revenues and expenses are recorded separately. We can calculate the revenues and expenses for the period January 2 through 8 as

Date	Revenues	Expenses
5	$ 300	$ 200
7	800	500
8	900	600
	Total $2,000	$1,300

We can now prepare an income statement. Its heading shows the name of the accounting entity, the title of the statement, and the period covered. The income statement reports revenues and expenses for the period and the difference between them, which is income:

GLENDALE MARKET

Income Statement
for the period January 2–8

Revenues......................	$2,000
Expenses	1,300
Income	$ 700

As the name suggests, "Retained Earnings" refers to the amount of income that has been retained in the entity. On January 13, Smith withdrew $600 of assets for his personal use. This reduced Retained Earnings by $600. Retained Earnings therefore became $100, calculated as follows:

Retained Earnings, January 2	$ 0
Income	+ 700
Withdrawal	− 600
Retained Earnings, January 13	$ 100

Assume that, in the remainder of January, Glendale Market had additional income of $800 and there were no additional withdrawals. Since retained earnings was $100 as of January 13, it would be $900 on January 31. Thus, the amount of retained earnings on a balance sheet is the total amount retained since the entity began operations.

The terms **profit, earnings, surplus,** and **income** all have the same meaning. They are the differences between the revenues of an accounting period and the expenses of that period. (Some people use the term **income** when they mean **revenue;** this can be confusing.) In later parts, we shall describe various revenue and expense items, such as sales revenue, interest revenue, salary expense, and rent expense. These explain in more detail the reasons for the change in Retained Earnings during a period.

Remember that the Equity section of the balance sheet reports the amount of capital that the entity has obtained from two sources:

- The amount paid in by the owner(s), which is called Paid-in Capital

- The amount of income that has been retained in the entity, which is called Retained Earnings

The two financial statements may be compared to two reports on a reservoir. One report may show how much water flowed through the reservoir during the period, and the other report may show how much water was in the reservoir as of the end of the period. Similarly, the income statement reports flows during a period of time, whereas the balance sheet reports status as of a point of time. Thus, the income statement may be called a flow report, and the balance sheet may be called a status report.

Note also that withdrawals by owners (which are called dividends in a corporation) are not expenses. They do not appear on the income statement and do not reduce income. However, they do decrease retained earnings.

KEY POINTS TO REMEMBER

The following diagram summarizes how assets are reported.

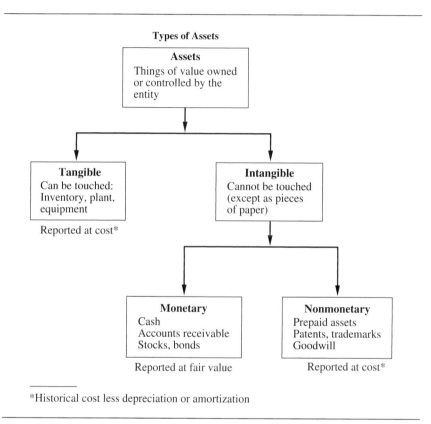

Types of Assets

Assets
Things of value owned or controlled by the entity

Tangible
Can be touched: Inventory, plant, equipment

Reported at cost*

Intangible
Cannot be touched (except as pieces of paper)

Monetary
Cash
Accounts receivable
Stocks, bonds

Reported at fair value

Nonmonetary
Prepaid assets
Patents, trademarks
Goodwill

Reported at cost*

*Historical cost less depreciation or amortization

- Current assets are cash and assets that are expected to be converted into cash or used up in the near future, usually within one year.

- Current liabilities are obligations due in the near future, usually within one year.

- Marketable securities are current assets; investments are noncurrent assets.

- A single liability may have both a current portion and a noncurrent portion.

- Equity consists of paid-in capital (which in a corporation is represented by shares of stock) plus earnings retained since the entity began. It does not report the market value of the stock. Retained Earnings is not cash; it is part of the owners' claim on the assets.

- Every accounting transaction affects at least two items and preserves the basic equation Assets = Liabilities + Equity. Accounting is a double-entry system.

- Some events are not transactions; they do not affect the accounting amounts. Examples in this part were a change in the value of land, goodwill that was not purchased, and a change in the entity from a proprietorship to a corporation.

- Other events affect assets and/or liabilities but have no effect on equity. Examples in this part were borrowing money, purchasing inventory, purchasing insurance protection, acquiring an asset, giving a mortgage, buying land, selling land at its cost, and repaying a bank loan.

- Still other events affect equity as well as assets and/or liabilities. Revenues are increases in equity resulting from operations during a period. Expenses are decreases. Their net effect is shown in the equity item called Retained Earnings. Equity also increases when owners pay in capital, and equity decreases when owners withdraw capital, but these transactions do not affect income.

- A sale has two aspects: a revenue aspect and an expense aspect. Revenue results when the sale is made, whether or not cash is received at that time. The related expense is the cost of the merchandise that was sold. The income of a period is the difference between the revenues and expenses of that period.

PART 3

Accounting Records
and Systems

This part describes
- The nature of the account and how entries are made to accounts
- The meaning of debit and credit
- Use of the ledger and the journal
- The closing process
- Items reported on the income statement
- Accounting with the computer

THE ACCOUNT

In Part 2 we recorded the effect of each transaction by changing the appropriate items on a balance sheet. Erasing the old amounts and writing in the new amounts would not be a practical method for handling the large number of transactions that occur in most entities. Instead of changing balance sheet amounts directly, accountants use a device called an **account** to record each change. In its simplest form, an account looks like a large letter "T," and it is therefore called a **T-account.**

The title of the account is written on top of the "T." As a matter of accounting custom, the name of an account is treated as a proper noun; that is, the first letter is capitalized. This is how a T-account looks at the beginning of an accounting period.

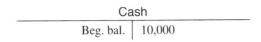

Cash	
Beg. bal.	10,000

From this, we can tell that the amount of cash at the beginning of the accounting period was $10,000. Note that, although the amounts are in dollars, the dollar sign is not used.

Transactions that affect the Cash account during the accounting period can either *increase* cash or *decrease* cash. Thus, one side of the T-account is for increases, and the other side is for decreases.

Increases in cash add to the beginning balance. Because the beginning balance is recorded on the left side of the T-account, increases in cash are recorded on the left side of the T-account. Decreases are recorded on the right side.

Example. The following changes in Cash are recorded in the T-account below:

    a. The entity received $300 cash from a customer.

    b. The entity borrowed $5,000 from a bank.

    c. The entity paid $2,000 cash to a supplier.

    d. The entity sold merchandise for $800 cash.

Cash			
Beg. bal.	10,000	2,000	(c)
(a)	300		
(b)	5,000		
(d)	800		

At the end of an accounting period, the increases are added to the beginning balance, and the total of the decreases is subtracted from it. The result is the **new balance.** The calculation of the new balance for the Cash account follows.

Cash

Beg. bal.	10,000	2,000	(c)
(a)	300		
(b)	5,000		
(d)	800		
Total	16,100	2,000	Total
Balance	14,100		

The amount of the Cash shown on the balance sheet at the end of the accounting period would be $14,100. The beginning balance of Cash in the next accounting period would also be $14,100.

RULES FOR INCREASES AND DECREASES

In the T-account for Cash, increases are recorded on the left side. This is the rule for all asset accounts; that is, increases in asset accounts are recorded on the left side.

Suppose Brown Company received $300 cash from Ellen Jones to settle her account receivable. In the following T-account, the increase in Brown Company's cash that results is recorded on the left side, as shown.

Cash

(Increases)	(Decreases)
Beg. bal. 10,000	
300	

Ellen Jones, a customer of Brown Company, paid $300 cash to settle the amount she owed. The Cash account increased by $300. Jones no longer owed $300, so the Accounts Receivable account decreased by $300. Accounts Receivable is an asset account. The dual-aspect concept requires that, if the asset account, Cash, increases by $300, the change in the other asset account, Accounts Receivable, must be a decrease of $300.

The decrease in accounts receivable is recorded on the right side of the Accounts Receivable account. This balances the left-side amount for the increase in Cash:

Accounts Receivable

(Increases)	(Decreases)
Beg. bal. 2,000	**300**

Another customer of Brown Company settled an $800 Account Receivable by paying $600 Cash and giving a note for $200. The effect on the accounts follows:

Cash	
(Increases)	(Decreases)
Beg. bal. 10,000	
300	
600	

Accounts Receivable	
(Increases)	(Decreases)
Beg. bal. 2,000	300
	800

Notes Receivable	
(Increases)	(Decreases)
Beg. bal. 1,000	
200	

As you can see, accounting requires that each transaction give rise to equal totals of left-side and right-side amounts. This is consistent with the fundamental equation: Assets = Liabilities + Equity.

An *increase* in any asset account is always recorded on the left side. Therefore, since the totals of left-side and right-side amounts must equal each other, a *decrease* in any asset must always be recorded on the right side.

Example. Black Company borrowed $700 from Federal Bank, signing a note. Black Company's Cash account increased by $700, and its Notes Payable account, which is a liability account, increased by the same amount. The $700 increase in Black Company's cash is recorded on the left side of its Cash account. In order to show equal totals of right-side and left-side amounts, the corresponding change in the Notes Payable account is recorded on the right side. These entries are as follows:

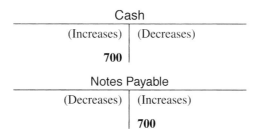

Because left-side and right-side amounts must have equal totals, and because increases in assets are always recorded on the left side, increases in liability accounts, such as Notes Payable, are always recorded on the right side.

Similarly, because *decreases* in assets are always recorded on the *right* side, *decreases* in liabilities are always recorded on the *left* side.

As the equation Assets = Liabilities + Equity indicates, the rules for equity accounts are the same as those for liability accounts—that is,

- Equity accounts increase on the right side.
- Equity accounts decrease on the left side.

One way to remember these rules is to visualize the two sides of the balance sheet. Asset accounts are on the *left* side of the balance sheet, and they increase on the left side. Liability and equity accounts are on the *right* side of the balance sheet, and they increase on the right side.

Sometimes, you will see a balance sheet on which Liabilities and Equity appear below the Assets section. This is a matter of preference on the part of the reporting entity.

DEBIT AND CREDIT

In the language of accounting, the left side of an account is called the **debit** side, and the right side is called the **credit** side. Thus, instead of saying that increases in cash are recorded on the left side of the Cash account and decreases are recorded on the right side, accountants say that increases are recorded on the debit side and decreases are recorded on the credit side.

Debit and **credit** are also verbs. To record an increase in cash, you debit the Cash account. To record a decrease in cash, you credit the Cash account. Instead of saying, "Record an amount on the left side of the Cash account," the accountant simply says, "Debit Cash."

The rules we just developed in terms of "left side" and "right side" can now be stated in terms of debit and credit:

Increases in assets are debits.
Decreases in assets are credits.
Increases in liabilities are credits.
Decreases in liabilities are debits.
Increases in equity are credits.
Decreases in equity are debits.

In everyday language the word "credit" sometimes means "good" and "debit" sometimes means "bad." In the language of accounting, "debit" means only left, and "credit" means only right. As you can see, debits are sometimes increases (when asset accounts are involved) and sometimes decreases (when liability or equity accounts are involved.)

The word "debit" is abbreviated as "Dr.," and the word "credit" is abbreviated as "Cr." In practice, these labels are not shown in the accounts, but we shall use them to help you fix them in your mind.

Because the total of the debit entries for any transaction should always equal the total of the credit entries, it is easy to check the accuracy with which bookkeeping is done. (We owe this ingenious arrangement to Venetian merchants, who invented it more than 500 years ago.)

INCOME STATEMENT ACCOUNTS

The income statement reports the revenues and the expenses of an accounting period and the difference between them, which is income. Revenues are increases in equity during a period, and expenses are decreases in equity.

For equity accounts, increases are recorded as credits. Because revenues are increases in equity, revenues are recorded as credits.

Similarly, decreases in equity are recorded as debits. Because expenses are decreases in equity, expenses are recorded as debits.

We can therefore complete the set of rules for making entries to accounts as follows:

- Increases in revenues are credits.

- Increases in expenses are debits.

These two rules, and the ones presented above, govern all accounting transactions. Although it may seem strange, increases in assets (which are generally considered to be "good things") and increases in expenses (which are sometimes considered to be "not so good") are debits. That's the way it has to be, in order to maintain the basic equation.

Earlier, we referred to the increase in Retained Earnings as "Income." From here on, we shall use the technically correct name: "Net Income." Net Income is the bottom line of the income statement. Various subtotals of income, such as Gross Income and Operating Income, are used in practice.

THE LEDGER AND THE JOURNAL

A group of accounts is called a **ledger.** There is no standard form, as long as there is space to record the debits and credits to each account. Exhibit 3.1 is the ledger of Glendale Market, the same company we examined in Part 2.

Exhibit 3.1

Glendale Market Ledger

Cash		Accounts Payable		Revenues	
10,000	2,000		2,000	**2,000**	300
5,000					800
300					900
800					

Accounts Receivable		Notes Payable		Expenses	
900			5,000	200	**1,300**
				500	
				600	

Inventory		Paid-In Capital		Retained Earnings	
2,000	200		10,000	**1,300**	**2,000**
2,000	500				
	600				

In practice, transactions are not recorded directly in the ledger. First, they are written in a record, such as Exhibit 3.2, called a journal. The record made for each transaction is called a **journal** entry.

As Exhibit 3.2 shows, for each journal entry, the account to be debited is listed first, and the Dr. amount is entered in the first of the two money columns. The account to be credited is listed below and is indented. The Cr. amount is entered in the second money column. If you are uncertain as to whether a particular account is to be debited or credited, you usually can find out by referring to the other account in the entry. For example, the entry to Accounts Receivable is an increase in an asset, which is a debit, so the entry to Revenues must be a credit.

Journal entries are transferred to the ledger by the process called **posting.** The entries through January 8 have already been posted, as indicated by the check mark opposite each.

To summarize, any transaction requires at least two changes in the accounts. These changes are recorded first in the journal. They are then posted to the ledger.

THE CLOSING PROCESS

The Revenues account in Exhibit 3.1 shows increases in Retained Earnings during the period, and the Expenses account shows decreases in Retained Earnings. The difference between revenues and expenses is the net income of the period. The net income for the period is an increase in the equity account, Retained Earnings. Net income is added to this account by a series of journal entries called **closing entries.**

In order to do this, we first must find the balance in the account that is to be closed. The balance in the Revenues account in Exhibit 3.1 is $2,000 (= $300 + $800 + $900). An entry (shown here in boldface) is made that reduces the balance in the account to be closed to zero and records the same amount in the Retained Earnings account. Because the Revenues account has a Cr. Balance, the entry that reduces revenues to zero must be on the other side; that is, it must be a Dr.

Therefore, the journal entry that closes the $2,000 balance in the Revenues account to Retained Earnings is

```
Dr. Revenues ...............2,000
    Cr. Retained Earnings ....        2,000
```

Using similar reasoning, the journal entry that closes the $1,300 balance in the Expenses account to Retained Earnings is

```
Dr. Retained Earnings.......1,300
    Cr. Expenses ............        1,300
```

Exhibit 3.2

JOURNAL

2006		Accounts		Dr.	Cr.
Jan.	2	Cash	√	10,000	
		Paid-in Capital	√		10,000
	3	Cash	√	5,000	
		Notes Payable	√		5,000
	4	Inventory	√	2,000	
		Cash	√		2,000
	5	Cash	√	300	
		Revenues	√		300
		Expenses	√	200	
		Inventory	√		200
	6	Inventory	√	2,000	
		Accounts Payable	√		2,000
	7	Cash	√	800	
		Revenues	√		800
		Expenses	√	500	
		Inventory	√		500
	8	Accounts Receivable	√	900	
		Revenues	√		900
		Expenses	√	600	
		Inventory	√		600

These two entries are then posted to the ledger in Exhibit 3.1.

To get ready for preparing the financial statements, the balance in each asset, liability, and equity account is calculated. (Revenue and expense accounts have zero balances because of the closing process.) **Journal** entries change the balance in the account. The *calculation* of the balance does not change the balance. Therefore, the calculation of a balance does not require a journal entry.

The balance sheet is prepared from the balances in the asset, liability, and equity accounts. The balance sheet for Glendale Market as of January 8 follows:

GLENDALE MARKET

Balance Sheet as of January 8

Assets		Liabilities and Equity	
Cash	$14,100	Accounts payable	$ 2,000
Accounts receivable	900	Notes payable	5,000
Inventory	2,700	Paid-in capital	10,000
		Retained earnings	700
Total Assets	$17,700	Total Liabilities and Equity	$17,700

The income statement is prepared from information in the Retained Earnings account, as follows:

GLENDALE MARKET

Income Statement
for the period January 2–8

Revenues	$2,000
Expenses	1,300
Net Income	$ 700

After the closing process, the revenue and expense accounts have zero balances. These accounts are therefore **temporary accounts.** They are started over at the beginning of each period. The asset accounts have debit balances, and the liability and equity accounts have credit balances; these balances are carried forward to the next period. Thus, income statement accounts are temporary accounts, and balance sheet accounts are **permanent accounts.**

Most entities report individual items of revenues and expenses (such as salary expense, maintenance expense, insurance expense) on their income statement. In order to do this, they set up an account for each expense item. Thus, if the income statement reported 2 revenue items and 10 expense items, there would be at least 12 revenue and expense accounts. We shall describe these accounts in later parts. The entries to them are made in exactly the same way as in the simple example given here.

Management needs more detailed information than is contained in the financial statements. For example, instead of one account, Accounts Receivable, it needs an account for each customer, so that the amount owed by each customer is known. Therefore, the ledger usually contains many more accounts than there are items on the financial statements.

Although you need to understand the bookkeeping process described in this part, you don't need to memorize the details. Our purpose is to show where the numbers in the financial statements come from. This helps you understand what the numbers mean.

A NOTE ON COMPUTERS

Most entities use a computer to do their accounting. The computer makes debit and credit entries according to exactly the same rules as those we have described. In this program, we must show the journal entries manually because what goes on inside the computer is not visible. The computer has the following advantages over the manual system we use in this program:

- The computer is much faster.

- The computer does not make copying errors. For example, when the computer writes a check, the amount of the check is always the amount credited to Cash and debited to another account. The amounts reported on the financial statement are the same as the balances in the accounts.

- The computer assures that debit entries always equal credit entries. It does not accept an entry in which this equality does not exist.

- Once an amount has been recorded in the computer, that amount may be used for several purposes. For example, an entry to Accounts Receivable is used in calculating the total amount in the Accounts Receivable account, the accounts of individual customers, and the amount reported on the balance sheet.

- The computer does not make arithmetic errors.

- The computer may require that certain rules be followed. For example, the credit entry for a check is always to the Cash account.

- The computer has built-in safeguards that help detect fraudulent and erroneous entries.

- In a company at several locations, an entry generated at one location can be transferred accurately to the central chart of accounts via the Internet. Companies have a chart of accounts that gives an account number for every possible transaction in the system. This can help to assure the tracking of information if it is necessary.

However, if the initial input to the computer is made by a person, an error made by that person may not be detected. For example, if a check is supposed to be for $962 and the bookkeeper keys in $926, the computer may not detect the error. (Some input errors can be avoided by the use of automatic input devices, such as scanners that read bar codes.)

Also, despite the built-in safeguards, the computer cannot detect certain types of fraudulent entries. As examples of multimillion-dollar errors reported in the press demonstrate, there is no guarantee that errors do not exist. Therefore, there must be an audit function to check the possibility of fraud or error. We will introduce some of the safeguards that are in place to prevent fraud later in this book.

Although the computer may perform most of the bookkeeping functions, it cannot replace the accountant. The accountant specifies the rules to be followed in routine transactions; however, as we shall see, some transactions require judgment as to the accounts affected and the amounts to be debited or credited. The accountant must tell the computer how to make these entries. If the accountant makes an incorrect decision, the accounts will be incorrect.

Most important is the fact that learning the financial accounting transactions and closing processes, as you are doing here, cannot be replaced by a computer. It is basic to the understanding of the underlying processes. Once you understand the mechanics behind and structure of the financial statements, using a computer to facilitate their completion makes sense.

KEY POINTS TO REMEMBER

- **Debit** refers to the left side of an account and **credit** to the right side.

- Increases in asset and expense accounts are debits.

- Increases in liability, equity, and revenue accounts are credits. Decreases are the opposite.

- For any transaction, debits must equal credits. For the whole set of accounts, debit balances must equal credit balances.

- Transactions are first recorded in a journal. Amounts are then posted to the accounts in a ledger.

- Revenue and expense accounts are temporary accounts. At the end of each accounting period, they are closed to Retained Earnings. The difference between the revenues of a period and the expenses of the period is the net income of the period. These revenues and expenses are reported on the income statement.

- Net income is the increase in Retained Earnings from operating performance during the period.

- Asset, liability, and equity accounts are permanent accounts. Their balances are carried forward to the next accounting period.

- Some revenues do not result in immediate cash inflows. Some expenses do not result in immediate cash outflows. Therefore, retained earnings **is not the same as cash!**

PART 4

Revenues and Monetary Assets

This part describes
- The accounting period
- Accrual accounting
- Three more of the nine basic accounting concepts:
  - Conservatism
  - Materiality
  - Realization
- How revenue items are measured
- How monetary assets are measured
- The days' sales uncollected ratio

In Part 3, we introduced the idea of Net Income. Net Income increases Retained Earnings. Retained Earnings is an item of equity on the balance sheet. Any increase in Retained Earnings is also an increase in equity. Net income results from the profitable operation of an entity. The amount of net income is one of the most important items of information that accounting reports. Net income is the difference between revenues and expenses. In this part, we describe how the revenue portion of net income is measured.

FISCAL YEAR

An income statement reports the amount of net income over a period of time. The period of time covered by one income statement is called the **accounting period.**

For most entities, the official accounting period is one year, referred to as the **fiscal year.** However, financial statements, called **interim statements,** usually are prepared for shorter periods. In Part 3, we prepared an income statement for Glendale Market for the period January 2 through January 8. This was an interim statement, and the accounting period was one week. For most entities, the accounting period is the **calendar year**—that is, the year that ends on the last day of the calendar, which is December 31.

Entities don't fire their employees and cease operations at the end of an accounting period. They continue from one accounting period to the next. The fact that accounting divides the stream of events into fiscal years makes the problem of measuring revenues and expenses in a fiscal year the most difficult problem in accounting.

ACCRUAL ACCOUNTING

On January 3, Glendale Market borrowed $5,000 from a bank. Its cash therefore increased and a liability increased, but its revenues did not change. Revenues are increases in equity. The receipt of $5,000 cash as a loan from the bank on January 3 therefore did not change equity.

On January 4, Glendale Market purchased $2,000 of inventory, paying cash. This was an increase in one asset and a decrease in another asset. Since equity was unchanged, the payment of cash on January 4 was not associated with an expense.

On January 8, Glendale Market sold merchandise for $900, and the customer agreed to pay $900 within 30 days. This transaction resulted in no change in cash. Revenue was $900. This revenue was not associated with a change in cash on January 8.

The examples show that revenues and expenses are not necessarily accompanied, at the same time, by changes in cash. Moreover, changes in cash are not necessarily coupled with corresponding changes in revenues or expenses. Increases and decreases in cash are changes in an asset account. Revenues and expenses are changes in an equity account.

Many individuals and some small businesses keep track only of cash receipts and cash payments. This type of accounting is called **cash accounting.** If you keep a record of your bank deposits, the checks you write, and the balance in your bank account, you are doing cash accounting. Cash accounting does not measure changes in equity.

Most entities, however, account for revenues and expenses, as well as for cash receipts and cash payments. This type of accounting is called **ac-**

crual accounting. Evidently, accrual accounting is more complicated than cash accounting, but accrual accounting does measure net income and, hence, changes in equity. The most difficult problems in accounting are problems of accrual accounting. Because net income is the change in equity and it measures the entity's financial performance, accrual accounting provides more information than cash accounting.

In order to measure the net income of a period, we must measure the revenues and expenses of that period, and this requires the use of accrual accounting. In this part, we describe the measurement of revenues. The measurement of expenses is described in later parts. First, we introduce three more accounting concepts: conservatism, materiality, and realization.

CONSERVATISM

Suppose that in January, Lynn Jones agreed to buy an automobile from Ace Auto Company; the automobile is to be delivered to Jones in March. Because Ace Auto Company is in the business of selling automobiles, it would be happy that Jones has agreed to buy one. Jones agreed in January to buy an automobile for delivery in March. Although Jones is likely to take delivery in March, it is possible that she will change her mind. The sale of this automobile therefore is uncertain.

Because in January the sale of this automobile is uncertain, accounting does not recognize the revenue in January. If Jones does accept delivery in March, accounting recognizes revenue in March. This is a conservative way to account for the transaction.

Recognize revenue when delivered

Increases in equity are recognized only when they are *reasonably certain.* To be conservative, decreases in equity should be recognized as soon as they probably occur. Suppose an automobile was stolen from Ace Auto Company in January, and the company waited until March to decide that the automobile was gone for good. Conservatism requires that the decrease in equity be recognized when it is *reasonably possible*—that is, in January.

The *conservatism concept* therefore has two parts:

1. Recognize *increases* in equity only when they are reasonably certain.
2. Recognize *decreases* in equity as soon as they are reasonably possible.

MATERIALITY

A brand new pencil is an asset of the entity that owns it. Every time an employee writes with a pencil, part of the asset's value decreases, and the entity's equity also decreases.

It would be possible, theoretically, to find out each day the number of partly used pencils and to make a journal entry showing the number of pencils that were used up and the corresponding "pencil expense" of that day. But it would be impractical to do this.

The accountant considers that the asset value of pencils was entirely used up at the time they were issued to the user. To do otherwise would be a waste of time. This solution is simple and practical, but less exact than the theoretically correct treatment.

The treatment of pencils is an example of the **materiality** concept. The materiality concept states that the accountant may disregard immaterial transactions. Material transactions or events are those that make a difference in understanding an entity's financial affairs. Deciding which transactions are material is a matter of judgment. There are no mechanical rules.

The other side of the coin is that the financial statements must disclose all material facts. For example, if a large fraction of a company's inventory is found to be worthless, the materiality concept requires that this fact be disclosed.

The materiality concept therefore has two parts:

1. Disregard trivial (i.e., unimportant) matters.
2. Disclose all important matters.

REALIZATION

Consider an entity that manufactures goods and then sells them. In accounting, the revenue from these goods is *recognized* at the time they are delivered to the customer, *not* at the time they are manufactured.

For example, Morgan Company manufactured an item in February and delivered it to a customer in March; the customer paid for it in April. Revenue should be recognized in March. If a company sells services rather than goods, revenue is recognized at the time the services are delivered.

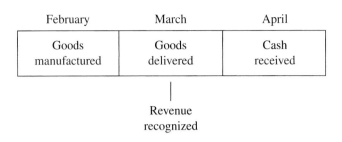

Goods (such as shoes) are tangible products. Services (such as repairing computers) are intangible products. Both goods and services are products. Thus, the general rule is that revenue from a product is recognized when the product is delivered.

At the time of delivery, revenue is said to be **realized.** The realization concept is that revenue is recognized and recorded in the period in which it is realized.

Examples. In January, Smith Company contracts to paint Herbert's house. The house is painted in February, and Herbert pays Smith Company in March. Smith Company should recognize revenue in February.

Gordon Company manufactures some imitation carrots in May. In June, it receives an order from Peter Rabbit, Esq., for one carrot. Gordon Company delivers the carrot in July. Peter Rabbit pays the bill in August and eats the carrot in September. Gordon Company would recognize revenue in July, which is after the order was received and before the cash was received.

Revenue is realized when a *sale* is completed by the delivery of a product. Because of this, the word "sales" is often used along with "revenue," as in the phrase "sales revenue."

A salesperson may say that he or she has "made a sale" when the order was written, even though the product is to be delivered at a future time. In accounting, writing a sales order is not a sale because the revenue has not yet been realized.

Revenue may be recognized (1) before, (2) during, or (3) after the period in which the cash from the sale is received. First, consider a case in which revenue is recognized in the same period as when the cash is received.

In January, Loren Company sold and delivered a motorcycle to Jerry Paynter, who paid $1,800 cash. In this example, revenue is recognized in the same month as the related cash receipt. In January, Loren Company sold another motorcycle for $3,800 and delivered it to Jean Matthews. Matthews agreed to pay for the motorcycle in 30 days. In this case, revenue is recognized in the month before the related cash receipt.

When revenue is recognized before the related cash receipt, as in the preceding transaction, the revenue is accompanied by the right to collect the cash, which is an Account Receivable. Thus, the entry for the sale of the motorcycle on credit was

```
Dr. Accounts Receivable.....3,800
    Cr. Revenue .............        3,800
```

When a customer pays an entity for a credit purchase, the entity records an increase in Cash and a corresponding decrease in Accounts Receivable. Thus, when Loren Company receives a check for $3,800 from Matthews in February, Loren Company makes the following entry:

```
Dr. Cash...................3,800
    Cr. Accounts Receivable ..        3,800
```

Revenue was not recognized in February.

Finally, consider the case in which revenue is recognized *after* the associated receipt of cash. In this case, the entity has an obligation to deliver the product. This obligation is a liability. It is listed on the right side of the balance sheet with the title **Advances from Customers.** (The terms "Deferred Revenue," "Precollected Revenue," and "Unearned Revenue" are sometimes used instead of "Advances from Customers.")

Example. In March, Maypo Company received $3,000 cash in advance from a firm to prepare an advertising brochure. Maypo Company would make the following entry in March to record this transaction.

```
Dr. Cash ......................3,000
    Cr. Advances from Customers ...        3,000
```

Maypo delivered the brochure in June. It therefore no longer had the liability Advances from Customers. In June, it would record the entry

```
Dr. Advances from Customers .....3,000
    Cr. Revenue ................        3,000
```

The customer's advance may provide for revenue that will be earned over several future accounting periods.

Example. Suppose, in 2005, a publisher received $50 for a magazine subscription, with the magazines to be delivered in 2006 and 2007. The entry for 2005 would be

```
Dr. Cash ......................50
    Cr. Advances from Customers ...    50
```

The amount of the liability at the end of 2005 would be $50. The entry for 2006 would be

```
Dr. Advances from Customers .....25
    Cr. Revenue .................    25
```

At the end of 2006, $25 would be reported as a liability on the balance sheet.

The entry for 2007 would be

```
Dr. Advances from Customers .....25
    Cr. Revenue .................    25
```

At the end of 2007, $0 would be reported as a liability on the balance sheet.

Note that the effect of recording these transactions is to assign the total subscription of $50 to the years in which the magazine will be delivered—$25 to each year.

SERVICE REVENUE

Revenue is recognized in the period in which services are delivered. If a landlord receives cash from a tenant in January and, in return, permits the tenant to use an apartment in February, March, and April, the landlord recognizes revenue in February, March, and April. This type of revenue is called **rental revenue.**

Example. In January, a tenant paid the landlord $2,400 cash covering rent for February, March, and April. The following table shows how much revenue the landlord would recognize each month and how much liability the landlord would report at the end of each month.

	Rental Revenue for the month	Liability at the end of month
January	$ 0	$2,400
February	800	1,600
March	800	800
April	800	0

When a bank lends money, it delivers a service; that is, the bank provides the borrower with the use of the money for a specified period of time. The bank earns revenue for the service it delivers during this period. This type of revenue is called **interest revenue.** In accordance with the realization concept, interest revenue is recognized in the period(s) in which the borrower has the use of the money. (The term "interest income" is sometimes used, but the amount actually is revenue, not income. Income is always a *difference* between revenue and expense.)

Interest revenue is similar to rental revenue. Banks *deliver* a service when they "rent" money; landlords *deliver* a service when they rent apartments. In both cases, revenue is realized in the period(s) in which the service is delivered.

To summarize, accountants recognize revenue in the month *before* the related cash receipt by crediting Revenues and debiting an asset account entitled Accounts Receivable.

Accountants recognize revenue in the month *after* the related cash receipt by debiting Cash and crediting a liability account when the cash is received. Revenue is recognized when the product is delivered in accordance with the realization concept.

There are exceptions to the principle that revenue is recognized when a product is delivered. They involve certain types of installment sales, certain long-term contracts, and a few other special situations. They are outside the scope of this introductory treatment.

AMOUNT OF REVENUE

The realization concept describes when revenue is recognized. The conservatism concept governs both *when* and *how much* revenue is recognized.

Suppose Loren Company sold a motorcycle to James Austin for $3,000 on credit, but Austin never paid the $3,000. Since Loren Company's assets decreased by one motorcycle but there was no actual increase in another asset, Loren Company's equity actually decreased as a result of this transaction. Loren Company did not realize revenue from this transaction.

Obviously, if Loren Company knew in advance that Austin would not pay for the motorcycle, Loren would not have delivered it. Although Loren would not knowingly sell a motorcycle to someone who is not going to pay, if some customers do not pay, there is a **bad debt.** Loren must take this possibility into account in measuring its income. It does this by estimating the amount of revenue that it is **reasonably certain** to receive from all its sales during the accounting period.

Recognizing only the amount of revenue that is reasonably certain to be received is required by the conservatism concept.

> *Example.* In 2005, Loren Company sold $500,000 of motorcycles to customers, all on credit. It estimated that 2% of these credit sales would never be collected; that is, they would become bad debts. Its estimate of bad debts for 2005 was $10,000 (0.02 × $500,000), and its increase in equity in 2005 was therefore only $490,000 ($500,000 − $10,000).

Loren Company recorded each sale as revenue at the time the motorcycles were delivered. In order to measure its increase in equity properly, it must decrease the total amount of the change in equity by $10,000.

After this decrease, the amount recognized as revenue is $490,000. This is the amount that is reasonably certain to be realized. This is in accordance with the conservatism concept.

Since the Accounts Receivable account includes amounts from customers who probably will never pay their bills, it overstates the real asset value. Thus, if the Loren Company decreases its equity by $10,000, it must also decrease its Accounts Receivable account by $10,000. Otherwise, the equality of Assets = Liabilities + Equity will not be maintained. However, accountants usually can't decrease the Accounts Receivable account directly because they don't know which customers will not pay their bills. Therefore, accountants usually set up a separate account, called **Allowance for Doubtful Accounts.** They record the estimated amount of bad debts as an increase in this account. Accounts Receivable, like all asset accounts, has a debit balance. Allowance for Doubtful Accounts, which is subtracted from Accounts Receivable, therefore must have the opposite balance—that is, a credit balance.

The Allowance for Doubtful Accounts is called a **contra-asset** account because it is subtracted from the asset, Accounts Receivable. Asset accounts have a debit balance, so a contra-asset account has a credit balance.

Although this decrease in equity theoretically resulted from the overstatement of revenue, accountants usually record it as an account called

Bad Debt Expense. The amount recorded as Bad Debt Expense would be $10,000. An increase in expense has the same effect on equity as a decrease in revenue.

The entry to record Loren Company's estimate that Bad Debt Expense should be increased by $10,000 and an Allowance for Doubtful Accounts of $10,000 should be established is

```
Dr. Bad Debt Expense ..........10,000
    Cr. Allowance for Doubtful Accounts  10,000
```

On December 31, 2005, Loren Company had $125,000 of Accounts Receivable before subtracting the Allowance for Doubtful Accounts. Loren Company's December 31, 2005, balance sheet would show

Accounts Receivable, gross	$125,000
Less: Allowance for Doubtful Accounts	− 10,000
Accounts Receivable, net	$115,000

If sometime in 2006, Loren Company recognizes it is never going to collect the $3,000 owed by Austin, it *writes off* the bad debt. It does this by decreasing Accounts Receivable and decreasing Allowance for Doubtful Accounts:

```
Dr. Allowance for Doubtful Accounts ..3,000
    Cr. Accounts Receivable .....      3,000
```

Loren Company's equity in 2005 was reduced by the estimated bad debts on sales made in 2005, but its equity in 2006 was not affected by this write-off of a bad debt. Since equity was decreased in 2005, it should not be decreased again for the same motorcycle. The write-off had no effect on the "Accounts Receivable, Net" item on the balance sheet, because both gross Accounts Receivable and the Allowance for Doubtful Accounts are reduced by the same amount.

MONETARY ASSETS

Monetary assets are cash and promises by an outside party to pay the entity a specified amount of money. Examples are accounts receivable, notes receivable, and bonds owned by the entity.

Monetary assets are usually reported on the balance sheet at the amounts that are reasonably certain to be received. By contrast, nonmonetary assets, such as buildings and equipment, are reported at their cost. This is in accordance with the asset-measurement concept.

DAYS' SALES UNCOLLECTED

Days' Sales Uncollected is the number of days of sales that are reported in Accounts Receivable at the end of the accounting period. Sales per day are total credit sales for the year divided by 365. The formula is

$$\text{Days' Sales Uncollected} = \frac{\text{Accounts Receivable}}{\text{Credit Sales} \div 365}$$

Thus, the Days' Sales Uncollected ratio, using the following data for Worley Company, would be

Accounts Receivable, December 31, 2005	$ 50,000
Credit sales for the year 2005	$365,000

$$\text{Days' Sales Uncollected} = \frac{\$50,000}{\$365,000 \div 365} = 50 \text{ days}$$

The Days' Sales Uncollected ratio indicates whether customers are paying their bills when they are due. If Worley Company expects customers to pay within 30 days from the date of the sale, the ratio of 50 days indicates that customers are not paying on time. (This is only a rough indication because it assumes sales are made evenly throughout the year, which is not the case with seasonal sales.)

KEY POINTS TO REMEMBER

- The official accounting period is called the fiscal year, but financial statements can be prepared for shorter periods. They are called interim statements.

- Accrual accounting measures revenues and expenses during an accounting period and the difference between them, which is net income. Accrual accounting is more complicated, but more useful, than accounting only for cash receipts and cash payments.

- The conservatism concept is as follows: Recognize increases in equity when they are reasonably certain, but recognize decreases as soon as they are reasonably possible.

- The materiality concept is as follows: Disregard trivial matters, but disclose all important matters.

- The realization concept is as follows: Revenue is usually recognized when goods and services are delivered.

- If revenue is recognized before the cash receipt, an asset, Accounts Receivable, is debited (increased). If cash is received before revenue is recognized, a liability, Advances from Customers, is credited (increased). The liability is debited (decreased) in the period(s) in which revenue is recognized.

- The equity and accounts receivable balances in a period are reduced by estimated bad debt losses. A Bad Debt Expense account is used to record the decrease in equity. When specific bad debts are later discovered, Accounts Receivable is reduced, but revenue is unaffected.

- The days' sales uncollected ratio is

$$\text{Days' Sales Uncollected} = \frac{\text{Accounts receivable}}{\text{Credit sales} \div 365}$$

It indicates whether customers are paying their bills on time.

PART 5

Expense Measurement; The Income Statement

This part describes
- The difference between "expense" and "expenditure"
- How the expenses of a period are measured
- The last of the nine basic accounting concepts; the matching concept
- The meaning of items reported on an income statement
- Methods of analyzing an income statement

In Part 4, you learned that the revenues recognized in an accounting period are not necessarily associated with the cash receipts in that period. If $1,000 of goods were delivered to a customer in August, and the customer paid cash for these goods in September, revenue would be recognized in August.

Revenues are increases in equity during an accounting period. Expenses are decreases in equity during an accounting period. Just as revenues in a period are not necessarily the same as cash receipts in that period, the expenses of a period are not necessarily the same as the cash payments in that period.

EXPENSE AND EXPENDITURE

When an entity acquires goods or services, it makes an **expenditure.** If, in August, Mogul Shop purchased goods for its inventory at a cost of $1,000, paying cash, it had an expenditure of $1,000 in August. It would record this transaction with the following journal entry:

```
Dr. Inventory..............1,000
    Cr. Cash ...............         1,000
```

If, in August, Mogul Shop purchased $2,000 of goods for inventory, agreeing to pay in 30 days, it had an expenditure of $2,000 in August. Accounts Payable, which is a liability account, increased. Mogul would record this transaction with the following journal entry:

```
Dr. Inventory..............2,000
    Cr. Accounts Payable .....         2,000
```

Thus, an expenditure results either in a decrease in the asset Cash or an increase in a liability, such as Accounts Payable. (Occasionally, an expenditure results in a decrease in an asset other than Cash. For example, when an old automobile is traded in for a new automobile, part of the expenditure is the decrease in the asset, Automobiles.)

Mogul Shop had expenditures of $3,000 in August for the purchase of goods for inventory. If $500 of these goods were sold in August, there was an **expense** in August of $500. The remaining $2,500 of goods are still in inventory at the end of August; they therefore are an **asset.** Thus, the expenditures of a period are either expenses of the period or assets at the end of the period.

Example. Mogul Shop sold the remaining $2,500 of goods in September. In September, it had an expense of $2,500, but it did not have any expenditure for these goods in September. If, in August, Mogul Shop paid an employee $2,000 cash for services rendered in August, it had both an expense and an expenditure of $2,000 for labor services in August.

When an asset is used up, or consumed, in the operations of the business, an expense is incurred. Thus, an asset gives rise to an expenditure when it is acquired and to an expense when it is consumed.

Example. Irwin Company purchased a supply of fuel oil in 2005, paying $10,000 cash. No fuel oil was consumed in 2005. In 2006, $8,000 of fuel oil was consumed and, in 2007, $2,000 was consumed. There was an expenditure in 2005, and there were expenses in 2006 and 2007.

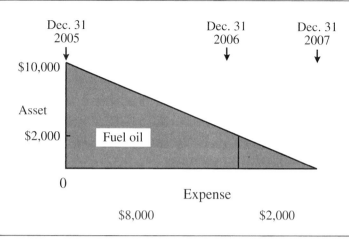

Between the time of their purchase and the time of their consumption, the resources of a business are assets. Thus, when fuel oil is purchased, there is an expenditure. The fuel oil is an asset until consumed. When consumed, it becomes an expense.

Example. Assume Irwin Company purchased a two-year supply of fuel oil in 2005, paying $10,000. None of it was consumed in 2005, $8,000 was consumed during 2006, and $2,000 was consumed in 2007. The balance sheet item for the asset Fuel Oil Inventory would show the following amounts:

As of December 31, 2005	$10,000
As of December 31, 2006	$ 2,000
As of December 31, 2007	$ 0

The item Fuel Oil Expense on the income statements would be as follows:

For the year 2005	$ 0
For the year 2006	$ 8,000
For the year 2007	$ 2,000

Over the life of a business, most expenditures will become expenses; however, in a single accounting period, expenses are not necessarily the same as expenditures.

UNEXPIRED AND EXPIRED COSTS

Expenditures result in costs. When inventory or other assets are acquired, they are recorded at their acquisition cost. Expenses are the cost of the resources used up in an accounting period. Costs that are consumed in a period are expenses. Costs that are represented by resources on hand at the end of the period are assets.

Costs that have been consumed are gone; they have **expired.** Costs of resources still on hand are **unexpired.** You will find it useful to think of expenses as expired costs and assets as unexpired costs.

To extend the example above, Irwin Company purchased $10,000 of fuel oil in 2005, consumed $8,000 of it in 2006, and consumed $2,000 of it in 2007. At the end of 2005, the total expenditure of $10,000 was an asset because none of the cost had expired. In 2006, $8,000 of the cost expired, and 48,000 was therefore an expense in 2006. At the end of 2006, $2,000 was an unexpired cost and therefore an asset. The remaining $2,000 expired in 2007, so it was an expense in 2007.

MATCHING CONCEPT

An important task of the accountant is to measure the net income of an accounting period. Net income is the difference between revenues and expenses of the period. Expenses are expired costs.

As you learned in Part 4, the concept governing the recognition of revenues of a period is the realization concept; revenue is recognized in the period in which goods or services are delivered.

The concept governing the recognition of expenses of a period is the **matching** concept. It states that *costs associated with the revenues of a period are expenses of that period.*

> *Example.* Consider an automobile that Bryan Company, an automobile dealer, purchased for $15,000 in March and sold (i.e., delivered) for $18,000 in May. At the end of March, the automobile was in the Bryan Company inventory, so its cost was unexpired. At the end of April, its cost was still unexpired. In May, Bryan Company recognizes $18,000 of revenue from the sale of this automobile. It must match the $15,000 of cost with the revenue from the sale of the same automobile. Thus, its expense in May is $15,000. The $18,000 of revenue and the $15,000 of expense relate to the same automobile. The expense *matches* the revenue.

OTHER ASSETS THAT WILL BECOME EXPENSES

When products are delivered, their costs are matched with revenues in the period in which the sale takes place. These costs become expenses of that period. This is one application of the matching concept. Other costs associated with activities of the current period are also expenses, even though they are not directly related to the products delivered in the period.

If expenditures were made in an earlier period, the unexpired costs are assets until the period in which the expense is recognized. We shall consider several examples. The first is an intangible asset.

A **tangible asset** has physical substance; an **intangible asset** does not have physical substance. Buildings, equipment, and inventories of goods are tangible assets. The protection provided by an insurance policy is an intangible asset.

The general name for intangible assets that will become expenses in a future period is **prepaid expenses.** The asset account may identify the particular type of prepaid expense. Thus, the name of the asset account that shows the cost incurred for insurance protection in future periods is Prepaid Insurance.

> ***Example.*** Bryan Company purchased a two-year insurance policy on December 31, 2005, for $2,000. The effect of this expenditure is a decrease in Cash and an increase in the asset Prepaid Insurance.

```
Dr. Prepaid Insurance......2,000
    Cr. Cash ..............          2,000
```

During 2006, Bryan Company used up half of this insurance protection, thereby incurring $1,000 of insurance expense. The effect on the accounts in 2006 is a decrease in the asset Prepaid Insurance and an increase in Insurance Expense.

```
Dr. Insurance Expense......1,000
    Cr. Prepaid Insurance ..        1,000
```

On December 31, 2006, the balance in the asset account, Prepaid Insurance, was $1,000.

During 2007, Bryan Company received the remaining $1,000 of insurance protection.

```
Dr. Insurance Expense......1,000
    Cr. Prepaid Insurance ..        1,000
```

On December 31, 2007, the amount of insurance protection has completely expired. The balance in the Prepaid Insurance account on that date therefore was zero.

Buildings and equipment also benefit future periods. They are assets like Prepaid Insurance and Prepaid Rent, except that they usually have a longer life and therefore benefit more future periods. The amount reported as an asset on the balance sheet is the unexpired cost as of the date of the balance sheet. Also, as with insurance and rent, the amount of building and equipment cost that is reported as an expense in each period is the amount of expired cost in that period.

The expired cost for buildings and equipment is called **Depreciation Expense.** If Bryan Company bought a machine for $5,000 and expected it to provide service for five years, the amount of expired cost in each year probably would be 1/5 of $5,000. In each of the five years, Depreciation Expense would be reported as $1,000. Accounting for depreciation is discussed in more detail in Part 7.

EXPENSES THAT CREATE LIABILITIES

We have described expenditures that first were assets and then became expenses as the costs expired. We now describe expenses for which the related expenditures are liabilities.

Amounts earned by the employees of Eastman Company for services performed in 2005 are expenses of 2005. If Eastman paid its employees one week after the week they worked, the amounts earned in the last week of 2005 would be a cash disbursement in 2006.

Assume that employees of Eastman Company earned $10,000 in the last week of 2005, for which they were paid in 2006. The $10,000 was both an expense and an expenditure in 2005. On December 31, 2005, Eastman Company owed its employees $10,000. It would report a liability of $10,000 on its December 31, 2005, balance sheet.

Liabilities for expenses incurred but not yet paid for are called **accrued liabilities.** Account titles may describe the nature of the liability—in this case, Accrued Salaries.

```
Dr. Salary Expense..........10,000
    Cr. Accrued Salaries .....          10,000
```

Employees are not paid the total amount they earn. Part of their salary is withheld by the employer, who pays it to the federal government for income taxes. Amounts are also deducted for social security taxes and for other reasons. We shall disregard these complications and assume that total earnings are paid in cash to the employees. In the last week of 2005, Eastman Company had a salary expense of $10,000, which was not paid to its employees.

Assume that, in January 2006, Eastman Company employees were paid the $10,000 owed them for work done in 2005. This payment decreases the liability Accrued Salaries. The journal entry for this transaction is

```
Dr. Accrued Salaries........10,000
    Cr. Cash ................        10,000
```

FRINGE BENEFITS

Many companies agree to pay employees a pension when they retire. Employees earn the right to their pension benefits when they work. Therefore, if an employee earns a $2,000 pension benefit in 2005 because he or she worked in 2005, the $2,000 is an expense in 2005. It is also a liability in 2005. The liability is called **Accrued Pensions.**

> *Example.* Joan Eaton earned a pension benefit of $2,000 in 2005. She had earned similar benefits in earlier years. The journal entry for this transaction is
>
> ```
> Dr. Pension Expense........2,000
>     Cr. Accrued Pensions .....        2,000
> ```

Joan Eaton retired on December 31, 2005. She will be paid a pension of $10,000 in 2006. The journal entry for the 2006 payment is

```
Dr. Accrued Pensions........10,000
    Cr. Cash ................        10,000
```

Many companies transfer amounts earned for pensions to an insurance company or a bank, which makes the actual payments. The effect on the company's financial position is nevertheless the same as that illustrated in the example's journal entries.

Many companies agree to pay for health care or other benefits to retired employees. These fringe benefits are called **Other Post Employment Benefits,** abbreviated OPEB. OPEB are accounted for in the same way as pensions; that is, the expense is incurred in the years in which the employee earns the right to them. The liability is also incurred in the years in which the employee earns the right to them. When the benefit is paid, there is no expense.

RENT EXPENSE

Eastman Company will pay its December rent of $5,000 in January. In December 2005, it records the Rent Expense of December and the related liability, Accrued Rent, by the following journal entry:

```
Dr. Rent Expense............5,000
    Cr. Accrued Rent .........           5,000
```

If, in January 2006, Eastman Company paid $5,000 to its landlord for the December 2005 rent, the journal entry in January would be

```
Dr. Accrued Rent............5,000
    Cr. Cash ................           5,000
```

Earlier, we saw that if rent is paid *prior* to the period in which the expense was incurred, the amount is first debited to Prepaid Rent, which is an asset account. As the previous frame indicates, if rent is paid *after* the period in which the expense was incurred, the credit is made to Accrued Rent, which is a liability account.

Prepaid Expenses are turned into expenses by a debit to the expense account and a credit to the asset account. Accrued Liabilities are discharged by a debit to Accrued Liabilities and a credit to Cash.

Of course, many items of expense are paid for in cash during the accounting period. Salaries of $90,000 earned in 2005 and paid in cash in 2005 are recorded in the following entry.

```
Dr. Salary Expense..........90,000
    Cr. Cash ................           90,000
```

LOSSES

Assets provide benefits to future periods. Suppose Bryan Company owned an uninsured machine that was destroyed by fire in 2005. The machine will not benefit future periods. The asset amount carried for the machine therefore expired in 2005, and this amount is recorded as an expense in 2005. Thus, although an asset does not provide benefits during a period, it is an expense of that period if its cost has expired for any reason. Such expenses are called **losses.** A loss is recorded as an expense in the period in which the loss occurs.

A loss is recorded as an expense if it is *reasonably possible* that the loss occurred, even though it is not certain. Thus, if a customer sues

Bryan Company in 2005, and if it seems reasonably possible that Bryan Company will lose the lawsuit, the estimated loss is recorded as an expense in 2005. This is in accordance with the conservatism concept, which requires expenses to be recognized when they are reasonably possible.

SUMMARY OF MATCHING CONCEPT

Three types of costs are expenses of the current period. The period in which revenues are recognized is determined first, according to the principles described earlier in this book. The associated costs are matched with those revenues. Costs are matched against revenues, not vice versa.

First, there are the costs of the goods and services that are *delivered* in the current period and whose revenues are recognized in that period.

Second, there are costs that are *associated with activities of the period.* The expenditures for these costs were made either in the current period or in an earlier period. If made in an earlier period, these amounts are assets on the balance sheet as of the beginning of the current period.

Third, there are losses that are *recognized in the current period.* These may recognize a reasonably possible decrease in an asset because of fire, theft, or other reasons. Or they may recognize a reasonably possible increase in a liability arising from events occurring in the period, such as a lawsuit.

The cash payments associated with any of these expenses may have been made in a prior period, in the current period, or in a future period, when the liabilities are paid.

The balance sheet at the beginning of a period reports assets obtained as a result of expenditures made in earlier periods. Part of these asset amounts will expire and therefore will be expenses of the current period. The remainder will be carried forward to future periods and will be reported as assets on the balance sheet at the end of the current period.

AN EXAMPLE OF MATCHING

Homes, Inc., is a company that buys and sells houses. Exhibit 5.1 describes some of its transactions during May, June, and July. These events relate to the sale of two houses, *House A* and *House B*. We will measure the income for Homes, Inc., for the month of June.

Delivery of the deed to a house is delivery of the ownership of the house. Exhibit 5.1 states that for *House A* this happened in June; therefore, revenue from the sale of *House A* is recognized in June.

Exhibit 5.1

TRANSACTIONS OF HOMES, INC.

Date	Event	Effects on Cash
May 2	Able agrees to buy House A from Homes, Inc., and makes a $16,000 down payment.	increase $16,000
May 15	Homes, Inc., pays $800 commission to the salesperson who sold House A (5% of cash received).	decrease $800
May	Homes, Inc., general expenses for May were $4,400 (assume for simplicity these were paid in cash in May).	decrease $4,400
June 2	Baker agrees to buy House B and makes a $24,000 down payment.	increase $24,000
June 5	Able completes the purchase of House A, paying $144,000 cash. Homes, Inc., delivers the deed to Able thereby delivering ownership of the house. (House A cost Homes, Inc., $140,000.)	increase $144,000
June 30	Homes, Inc., pays $1,200 commission to the salesperson who sold House B.	decrease $1,200
June	Homes, Inc., general expenses for June were $4,000	decrease $4,000
July 2	Homes, Inc., pays $7,200 additional commission to the salesperson who sold House A.	decrease $7,200
July 3	Baker completes the purchase of House B, paying $216,000 cash. Homes, Inc., delivers the deed to Baker, thereby delivering ownership of the house. (House B cost Homes, Inc., $200,000.)	increase $216,000
July 30	Homes, Inc., pays $10,800 commission to the salesperson who sold House B.	decrease $10,800
July	Homes, Inc., general expenses for July were $4,800	decrease $4,800

The amount of revenue for House A is measured by two transactions:

Date	Transaction	Amount
May 2	Down payment	$ 16,000
June 5	Final payment	144,000
	Revenue from House *A*	$160,000

Certain costs are associated with the total revenue from the sale of *House A* of $160,000 in June. One of these costs was the cost of *House A*, which was $140,000.

Two of the cash payments related specifically to the sale of *House A*:

Date	Transaction		Amount
May 15	Commission		$ 800
July 2	Commission		7,200
		Total	$8,000

The matching concept requires that the costs associated with the revenues of a period be recognized as expenses of that period. Therefore, the two commissions associated with *House A*, totaling $8,000, should be recognized as expenses in June, even though they were not paid in that month.

In accordance with the realization concept, the $24,000 down payment received on *House B* in June was not revenue in June. It will be revenue in July. Because Homes, Inc., has an obligation to deliver the house, the $24,000 is a liability on the balance sheet at the end of June.

The matching concept says that general costs of operations during any period are expenses of that period. Thus, the $4,000 general costs of operations in June are expenses in June.

The income statement for Homes, Inc., for the month of June, applying the realization concept and the matching concept, follows.

HOMES, INC.

Income Statement for June

Sales revenue	$160,000 (= $16,000 + $144,000)
Expenses:	
Cost of house	$140,000
Commission expense	8,000 (= $800 + $7,200)
General expenses	4,000
Total expenses..................	152,000
Income	$ 8,000

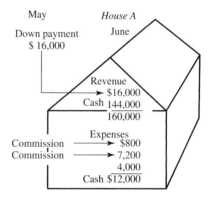

According to Exhibit 5.1, cash transactions in June were

June	Event	Cash Increases	Cash Decreases
2	Down payment on House *B*	$ 24,000	
5	Final payment on House *A*	144,000	
30	Commission on House *B*		$1,200
	General expenses for June		4,000

In June, Cash increased by a net amount of $162,800. This increase had no relation to the $8,000 net income for June.

THE INCOME STATEMENT

The equity section of a balance sheet shows the two sources of equity capital: (1) the capital supplied by equity investors (i.e., proprietors, partners, shareholders), which is called Paid-in Capital, and (2) that portion of the earnings resulting from profitable operations that have been retained in the entity, which is called Retained Earnings.

The amount added to Retained Earnings as a result of profitable operations during a period is the income of the period. An income statement explains how this income was earned.

The income statement is also called a Profit and Loss, or Earnings, statement. There is no standard format for an income statement. The lower portion of Exhibit 5.2 shows one common format. The first item on this income statement is Sales Revenue, which is the amount of products (i.e., goods and services) delivered to customers during the period.

The item on the second line is labeled Cost of Sales. It reports the cost of the goods or services whose revenue is reported on the first line. This is an example of the matching concept.

The difference between sales and cost of sales is called Gross Margin. Thus,

Gross margin = Sales revenue − Cost of Sales

Operating expenses are subtracted from Gross margin, giving the item **Income Before Taxes.** In accordance with the matching concept, these expenses include costs related to the current period and costs that do not benefit future periods (i.e., losses).

The next item on Exhibit 5.2, provision for income taxes, is shown separately because it is an especially important expense. These taxes relate to the income tax payable on the current period's income, not the income tax paid in that period.

The final item (the bottom line) on an income statement is called **Net** Income (or **Net** loss, if expenses are larger than revenues).

To arrive at net income, **dividends** are not subtracted from revenues. Dividends are not an expense. Dividends are a distribution of earnings to shareholders.

A PACKAGE OF ACCOUNTING REPORTS

An income statement is a summary of Retained Earnings that have been generated during a fiscal year. Also, an income statement reports certain changes in Retained Earnings that have taken place between two balance sheets.

Thus, a useful accounting "report package" consists of a balance sheet at the *beginning* of the accounting period, an income statement *for* the period, and a balance sheet *at the end* of the period.

Exhibit 5.2

A "PACKAGE" OF ACCOUNTING REPORTS
($000 OMITTED)

GARSDEN COMPANY

Condensed Balance Sheet as of December 31, 2005		Condensed Balance Sheet as of December 31, 2006	
Assets		**Assets**	
Current assets	$23,024	Current assets	$22,651
Buildings and equipment	14,100	Buildings and equipment	13,412
Other assets	1,662	Other assets	2,176
Total Assets	$38,786	Total Assets	$38,239
Liabilities and Equity		**Liabilities and Equity**	
Liabilities	$14,622	Liabilities	$12,343
Equity:		Equity:	
Paid-in capital	12,256	Paid-in capital	12,256
Retained earnings	11,908	Retained earnings	13,640
Total Liabilities and Equity	$38,786	Total Liabilities and Equity	$38,239

Income Statement
For the Year 2006

Sales Revenue	$75,478
Less cost of sales	52,227
Gross margin	23,251
Less operating expenses	10,785
Income before taxes	12,466
Provision for income taxes	6,344
Net income	$ 6,122

Statement of Retained Earnings

Retained earnings, 12/31/01	$11,908
Add Net income, 2002	6,122
	18,030
Less dividends	4,390
Retained earnings, 12/31/02	$13,640

Exhibit 5.2 shows a financial report package consisting of an income statement and two balance sheets. The exhibit shows that Retained Earnings on December 31, 2005, was $11,908,000. During 2006, profitable operations resulted in net income of $6,122,000, which increased Retained Earnings by this amount. (Net income is the **bottom line** on the income statement.)

Retained Earnings was decreased by $4,390,000, representing a distribution to the shareholders in the form of dividends. As a result, the total Retained Earnings on December 31, 2006, was $13,640,000 (= $11,908,000 + $6,122,000 − $4,390,000).

Remember that dividends are a distribution of earnings to owners. Dividends are *not* an expense.

The "package" of required financial statements includes a Statement of Cash Flows. This statement is described in Part 9.

INCOME STATEMENT PERCENTAGES

In an analysis of a business's performance, **percentages** of certain income statement items are usually calculated. The base (i.e., 100%) is **Sales Revenue.** One percentage is the **gross margin percentage,** which is found by dividing Gross margin by Sales revenue.

The gross margin percentage for Garsden Company in 2006 would be

$$\frac{\text{Gross Margin}}{\text{Sales Revenue}} = \frac{\$23,251}{\$75,478} = 31\%$$

An even more important percentage is the **Net income percentage,** which for Garsden Company is

$$\frac{\text{Net Income}}{\text{Sales Revenue}} = \frac{\$6,122}{\$75,478} = 8\%$$

The net income of many American manufacturing corporations is roughly 5–10% of sales revenue, but there is a wide variation from company to company.

REVIEW OF BASIC CONCEPTS

The nine basic concepts described in this book appear in the following list. These concepts are not stated as such in the accounting literature, but most accountants would agree that they are the basic underpinnings of accounting.

Dual-aspect concept: Assets = Liabilities + Equity
Money-measurement concept: Accounting reports only facts that can be expressed in monetary amounts.

Entity concept: Accounts are kept for an entity as distinguished from the persons associated with that entity.

Going-concern concept: Accounting assumes that an entity will continue to operate indefinitely and that it is not about to be sold or liquidated.

Asset-measurement concept: Accounting focuses on the fair value of monetary assets; nonmonetary assets are reported at an amount based on cost.

Conservatism concept: Revenues are recognized when they are reasonably certain. Expenses are recognized when they are reasonably possible.

Materiality concept: Disregard insignificant matters. Disclose all important matters.

Realization concept: Revenues are recognized when goods or services are delivered.

Matching concept: The expenses of a period are costs associated with the revenues or activities of the period.

KEY POINTS TO REMEMBER

- Expenditures are made when goods or services are acquired. If these goods or services are used up during the current period, they are expenses of the period. If not used up, they are assets at the end of that period. These assets will become expenses in future periods as they are used up.

- Some expenditures result in liabilities that will be paid in future periods. An example is accrued salaries.

- Expenses are expired costs. Assets are unexpired costs.

- The matching concept is as follows: Costs associated with the revenues or activities of a period are expenses of the period.

- Expenses of a period are (1) cost of the products (i.e., goods and services) that were delivered to customers during the period; (2) other expenditures that benefit operations of the period; and (3) losses—that is, decreases in assets from fire, theft, and other unusual reasons and increases in liabilities from unusual events, such as lawsuits.

- The income statement summarizes revenues and expenses of the period. Its bottom line, or net income, shows the increase in equity resulting from activities during the period.

- Dividends are a distribution of earnings to shareholders. Dividends are not expenses.

- Retained Earnings at the beginning of the period + Net Income − Dividends = Retained Earnings at the end of the period.

- Percentages are calculated for various income statement items, especially gross margin and net income, taking sales revenue as 100%.

PART 6

Inventories and Cost of Sales

This part describes
- How the cost of sales is calculated
- Methods of arriving at inventory amounts
- When inventory amounts on the balance sheet are reduced
- How inventory is measured in a manufacturing company
- The distinction between product costs and period costs
- How overhead rates are calculated

FINDING COST OF SALES

In the income statement in Part 5, the first item subtracted from sales revenue was called **Cost of Sales.** It is the cost of the same products whose revenues are included in the sales amount. This is an example of the matching concept. (Some businesses call this item **Cost of Goods Sold.**) In most businesses, the cost of sales is the largest item of expense, amounting to as much as 85% of sales revenues in a profitable supermarket and 60–70% in a profitable manufacturing company.

In some entities, matching cost of sales and sales revenue is easy. For example, an automobile dealer keeps a record of the cost of each automobile in its inventory. If the dealer sold two automobiles during a given month, one for $18,000 that had cost $16,000 and the other for $10,000 that had cost $7,500, sales revenue for the period would be recorded as $28,000 and cost of sales as $23,500. This is the **specific identification method.**

> ***Example.*** A dealer sold an automobile costing $16,000 for $18,000 cash. The journal entry that records the effect of this transaction solely on the Sales Revenue and Cash accounts follows:

```
Dr. Cash ................18,000
     Cr. Sales Revenue ......        18,000
```

> The journal entry that records the effect of this transaction solely on the Inventory and Cost of Sales accounts is

```
Dr. Cost of Sales .........16,000
     Cr. Inventory ..........        16,000
```

A dealer that sells televisions might keep a record of its inventory of each type of television, something like the following:

Item: Television #602, Cost $200 each

Date	Receipts		Shipments to Customers		On Hand	
	Quantity	Cost	Quantity	Cost	Quantity	Cost
May 1					4	800
6			1	200	3	600
10	10	2,000			13	2,600
13			6	1,200	7	1,400
31			2	400	5	1,000
Totals	10	2,000	9	1,800	5	1,000

This is called a **perpetual inventory** record. "Receipts" are increases in inventory, and "Shipments to Customers" are decreases in inventory.

Information in the perpetual inventory records corresponds to that in the Inventory account. From the previous frame, we see that the beginning balance for Television #602 in the Inventory account on May 1 was $800.

There were receipts during May of $2,000, which added to Inventory; these were a Dr. to the Inventory account. Shipments during May decreased inventory by $1,800, which were a Cr. to the Inventory account. This decrease in inventory was cost of sales in May, which was $1,800.

Using the *totals* in the perpetual inventory record, the inventory transactions for May would be recorded in the T-accounts as follows. (The inventory purchases were on credit.)

Inventory		
Beg. bal.	800	1,800
	2,000	

Cost of Sales	
1,800	

Accounts Payable	
	2,000

Televisions that cost $1,800 were sold in May for $2,500. The following partial income statement reflects this, assuming these were the only items sold.

Income Statement
May

Sales revenue	$2,500
Cost of sales	1,800
Gross margin	700

If an entity has a perpetual inventory, as illustrated, finding cost of sales in a month is easy. Thanks to computers, many more companies use the perpetual inventory method. We shall next show how to deduce cost of sales in a business that does not have this record. This method is the process of **deduction.**

Many stores, such as hardware stores, carry so many relatively low-value items that keeping a perpetual inventory record for each separate item is not practical. When the salesperson rings up a sale on the cash register, a record is made of the sales revenue but not the cost of sales. (In a computerized environment, the cash register—or point-of-sale terminal—records both sales revenue and the cost of sales.) If a hardware store does not keep a record of the cost of each item in inventory, it must deduce cost of sales by an indirect method.

Items in a hardware store's **beginning inventory** on January 1, 2005, were available for sale during 2005. Additional items *purchased* and placed on the shelves during 2005 were also available for sale during 2005. Therefore, the **goods available for sale** in a period are the sum of the beginning inventory plus the purchases during the period.

For example, assume that on January 1, 2005, Cantal Hardware had an inventory that cost $200,000. During 2005, it purchased $600,000 of additional merchandise. The cost of goods available for sale in 2005 was $800,000.

Accountants *assume* that goods available for sale during a period either are in inventory at the end of the period or were sold. Thus, if goods costing $800,000 were available for sale during 2005 and goods costing $300,000 were in inventory on December 31, 2005, cost of sales in 2005 is *assumed* to be $500,000.

At the end of each accounting period, all goods currently on hand are counted. This process is called **taking a physical inventory.** Since its purpose is to find the cost of the goods that were sold, each item is reported at its cost. In order to determine the ending inventory of one period and the beginning inventory of the next period, only one physical inventory must be taken, because the ending inventory on December 31, 2005, is also the beginning inventory on January 1, 2005.

Entities that use the perpetual inventory method count physical inventory at least annually. This inventory may reveal that the actual ending inventory is lower than is indicated in the perpetual inventory records because of theft, errors in record keeping, or items that have been discarded. If so, the ending inventory is reduced by a credit entry. The offsetting debit entry is to an expense account usually called "Loss on Inventory."

In the deduction method, goods not in inventory are assumed to have been sold. Sometimes goods are stolen, damaged, or spoiled. Therefore, the assumption that goods not in the closing inventory were sold is not necessarily valid. However, steps are taken to discover and record this **shrinkage.**

To summarize, many entities do not keep track of individual items in inventory. They find their cost of sales by the process of deduction. This requires a physical inventory. An automobile dealership finds its cost of sales directly from its physical inventory records.

Entities that must calculate cost of sales do so by subtracting the ending inventory from the total goods available, as in the following table:

Cost ($000 omitted)	
Beginning inventory	$200
Purchases	600
Total goods available	800
Ending inventory	300
Cost of sales.................................	500

The same situation is shown in the following diagram.

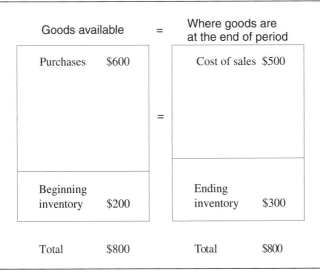

INVENTORY VALUATION: ASSUMPTIONS

In the preceding example, we assumed that all units of a given item, such as Television #602, were purchased at the same cost. Actually, the cost of goods purchased at different times may differ. For example, because inflation leads to increases in cost, the cost of goods purchased recently may be higher than the cost of the same goods purchased some time ago. In the following section, we describe the three principal methods of finding cost of sales and ending inventory in such a situation.

Lewis Fuel Company deals in fuel oil. Its inventory and purchases during April are shown in Exhibit 6.1. The "Unit Cost" shows that fuel oil entered the inventory at different unit costs during April.

What unit cost should we assign to the ending inventory? There are three choices: (1) we could assume that the older fuel oil was sold, leaving the newer fuel oil in inventory; (2) we could assume that the newer fuel oil

Exhibit 6.1

LEWIS FUEL COMPANY

	Quantity	Unit Cost	Total Cost
Beginning inventory, April 1	400	1.00	400
Purchases, April 10	300	1.10	330
Purchases, April 20	300	1.20	360
Total goods available	1,000		1,090
Ending inventory, April 30	600		?
Cost of sales, April			?

FIFO METHOD

Goods available...		$1,090
Ending inventory:		
300 units @ $1.20 = ...	$360	
300 units @ $1.10 = ...	330	
Total 600 units		690
Cost of sales..		$ 400

LIFO METHOD

Goods available...		$1,090
Ending inventory:		
400 units @ $1.00 = ...	$400	
200 units @ $1.10 = ...	220	
Total 600 units		620
Cost of sales..		$ 470

AVERAGE-COST METHOD

Average cost of

$$\frac{\$1,090}{1,000} = \$1.09 \text{ cost per unit}$$

Goods available......................................	$1.090
Ending inventory: 600 units @ $1.09 =.......	$654
Cost of sales: 400 units @ $1.09 =..............	$436

was sold, leaving the older fuel in inventory; or (3) we could assume that a mixture of old and new oil was sold.

Because the fuel oil has been mixed together in the storage tank, we do not have a record of the cost of the specific quantities of fuel oil actually sold during the month. Therefore, the solution is not clear-cut.

FIRST-IN, FIRST-OUT (FIFO) METHOD

In this situation, many companies make the **first-in first-out (FIFO)** assumption, *for financial accounting purposes only*. They assume that the goods that came into the inventory first are the first to move out.

In the FIFO method, we assume that the older fuel oil was sold during the month and that the newer fuel oil remains in the ending inventory. Therefore, in Exhibit 6.1, the ending inventory of 600 units of fuel oil is assumed to be the most recently purchased fuel oil—namely, the 300 units that were purchased on April 20 at $1.20 per unit and the 300 units purchased on April 10 at $1.10 per unit.

The ending inventory under the FIFO method therefore is

$$
\begin{array}{ll}
300 \text{ units @ } \$1.20 = \$360 \\
\underline{300 \text{ units @ } \$1.10 = \$330} \\
600 \text{ units} \qquad\qquad \$690
\end{array}
$$

The cost of goods available for sale was $1,090. We enter this amount in our calculation and subtract the ending inventory of $690 from it. The difference is the FIFO cost of sales, which is $400. Remember, this is done *for financial accounting purposes only*. It does not mean that the goods actually flowed through inventory in this order.

LAST-IN, FIRST-OUT (LIFO) METHOD

The FIFO method assumes that the oldest unit—that is, those first in, were the first to be sold; that is, that they were the first out. The **LIFO** method assumes the opposite—namely, that the newest units, which were the last in, were the first to be sold; that is, that they were first out, hence the name last-in, first-out.

Because the LIFO method assumes that the last units purchased were the first ones to be sold, the ending inventory is assumed to consist of any remaining units in beginning inventory, plus the earliest units purchased. In Exhibit 6.1, the ending inventory was 600 units, and in the LIFO method these 600 units are assumed to be the 400 units in beginning inventory plus 200 of the 300 units purchased on April 10.

Under the LIFO method, the amount available for sale remains $1,090; the ending inventory is

$$400 \text{ units @ } \$1.00 = \$400$$
$$\underline{200 \text{ units @ } \$1.10 = \$220}$$
$$600 \text{ units} \qquad\qquad \$620$$

and the cost of sales is $1,090 - $620 = $470.

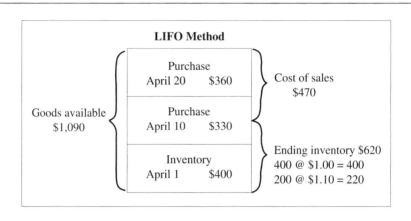

AVERAGE-COST METHOD

The third method is the **average-cost** method. It calculates the cost of both the ending inventory and the cost of sales at the average cost per unit of the goods available. In Exhibit 6.1, the number of units available in April was 1,000, and the total cost of these goods was $1,090, so the average cost per unit was $1.09.

```
Using the average cost of $1.09 per unit, the
ending inventory is
```
600 units @ $1.09 = $654.
```
Cost of sales is therefore
```
400 units @ $1.09 = $436.

COMPARISON OF INVENTORY METHODS

Most businesses try to sell their oldest goods first, so the goods that were first out are likely to be the goods first in. The FIFO method reflects this practice.

From Exhibit 6.1, we see that cost of sales under FIFO was 400 and under LIFO it was $470. Cost of sales was higher under LIFO.

In most companies, during periods of rising prices (i.e., inflation) the same relationship holds; that is, cost of sales is higher under LIFO than under FIFO.

In calculating income taxes, cost of sales is one of the items subtracted from revenue in order to find taxable income. Assume the revenue of Lewis Fuel Company was $1,000. Disregarding other expenses, if cost of sales was $470, taxable income would be $530. If cost of sales was $400, taxable income would be $600, which is $70 higher.

Thus, the higher the cost of sales, the lower the taxable income. The lower the taxable income, the lower the income tax based on that income.

Companies usually prefer to pay as low an income tax as they legally can. Therefore, they prefer the method that results in the higher cost of sales. If prices are rising, this is usually the LIFO method.

Any of the methods described is permitted in calculating taxable income in the United States. However, a company cannot switch back and forth between methods from one year to the next. In many countries, the LIFO method is not permitted.

INVENTORY VALUATION: ADJUSTMENT TO MARKET

We have assumed so far that inventory is recorded at its cost. Suppose, however, that the fair value (i.e., market value) of the inventory falls below its original cost. The conservatism concept requires that we reduce the inventory account to the lower amount.

For this reason, if the fair value of an item of inventory at the end of an accounting period is lower than its original cost, the item is "written down" to its fair value. For example, if an item whose original cost was $100 and whose current fair value is $80, its inventory amount should be written down by $20. (This is an exception to the general rule that non-monetary assets are reported at cost.)

In writing down inventory, the Inventory account is credited, and Cost of Sales is debited.

Example. If inventory is written down by $20, the appropriate journal entry is

```
Dr. Cost of Sales..........20
    Cr. Inventory .........          20
```

INVENTORY IN A MANUFACTURING COMPANY

A company that sells finished goods that it purchased from other vendors is a merchandising company. A company that converts raw materials into finished goods and then sells these goods is a manufacturing company. Retail stores, wholesalers, and distributors are merchandising companies. A company that makes shoes is a manufacturing company.

A merchandising company buys its goods in salable form; it receives an invoice showing the cost for each item. The costs on these invoices are the amounts used to record the additions to inventory. A manufacturing company adds value to the raw material it buys; it must include these **conversion costs** in its inventory and cost of sales. Measuring inventory and cost of sales is therefore more complicated in a manufacturing company.

In a *manufacturing* company, the cost of a finished product consists of three elements:

- Cost of *materials* used directly in that product

- Cost of *labor* used directly on that product

- A fair share of *overhead,* or general, costs associated with the production process

Some materials, such as oil for lubricating machinery, are not used directly on a product. The materials that are used *directly* in the product are called direct materials. Similarly, the labor used directly to make the product is called direct labor.

Production overhead consists of all other production costs—that is, costs that are not direct materials or direct labor. In some manufacturing companies, computer and automated machine tools replace workers, so direct labor cost is relatively small. These companies combine labor costs and production overhead costs into a single item called **Other Production Costs.**

The three elements of production cost—**direct labor, direct materials,** and **overhead**—are added together to determine the total cost of the finished product. Until the product is sold, this amount is held in the Inventory account. When the product is sold, this amount becomes Cost of Sales. Thus, if a product requires $5 of direct labor, $7 of direct materials, and $3 of overhead, the product will be costed at $15 as long as it is in the Inventory account. When it is sold, Cost of Sales will be $15.

The process of assigning production costs to products is called **cost accounting.** The assignment of costs to various services in banks, schools, hotels, and all types of service organizations also involves cost accounting. We shall describe some of its major aspects. The details of **cost accounting** and the related uses of cost data by managers is beyond the scope of this introductory book.

PRODUCT COSTS AND PERIOD COSTS

Costs are divided into two categories; they are treated differently for purposes of accounting:

1. **Product costs**—costs associated with the production of products
2. **Period costs**—costs associated with the sales and general activities of the accounting period

For example, the cost of heating the offices of the sales department would be considered a period cost. The cost of heating the production plant itself would be a product cost.

Overhead costs that are classified as product costs are added to direct labor costs and direct material costs to find the total cost that is added to the Inventory account. If Lee Shoe Company incurred $480,000 of production overhead costs in the year 2006, these costs would be added to inventory by this journal entry:

```
Dr. Inventory ................480,000
    Cr. Various overhead accts...      480,000
```

Costs are moved from Inventory to Cost of Sales when the products are sold. If, in the year 2006, Lee Shoe Company sold shoes with direct material and labor costs of $1,000,000 and overhead costs of $400,000, the entry would be

```
Dr. Cost of Sales..........1,400,000
    Cr. Inventory ...........      1,400,000
```

This entry included only $400,000 of overhead costs, although $480,000 of overhead costs were actually incurred in the year 2006. The Cost of Sales amount was not the same as the amount of cost actually incurred in the year 2006.

Period costs reduce income in the period in which the costs were incurred. Product costs reduce income in the period in which the product is sold, which often is a later period.

OVERHEAD RATES

By definition, direct material and direct labor costs can be traced directly to the products for which they were incurred; the cost accounting system does this. However, production overhead, which is an indirect cost, cannot be so traced. The cost of heating a shoe factory cannot be traced directly to the cost of manufacturing each pair of shoes made in the factory. Assigning these **indirect costs** to products requires the use of an **overhead** rate.

The overhead rate is a rate per direct labor dollar, per direct labor hour, per machine hour, or another measure of volume. If Lee Shoe Company expected to incur $480,000 of production overhead costs in the year 2006, and it expected that direct labor costs in the year 2006 would be $400,000, it would establish an overhead rate of $1.20 per direct labor dollar.

This overhead rate would be used to find the overhead cost of each pair of shoes worked on. If an actual pair of shoes required $10 of direct labor cost, its overhead cost would be recorded as $12.

If a certain pair of shoes required $20 of direct material cost, $15 of direct labor cost, and overhead at a cost of $1.20 per dollar of direct labor, its total cost would be $53 = $20 + $15 + ($15 * 1.2). The Inventory cost of these shoes would be $53. When they were sold, the Cost of Sales of these shoes would be $53.

Although $53 is reported as the "actual" cost of this pair of shoes, it cannot represent the actual overhead cost. By definition, it is not possible to determine the actual indirect cost of a product. The overhead rate does charge products with what is believed to be a *fair share* of their cost. For this reason, the process of allocating overhead costs to products is more complex than the scope of this book.

There are several other methods of assigning overhead costs to products. One of these, called **activity-based costing,** assigns indirect or overhead costs on the basis of the relative activities that cause costs. This process looks at the *cost drivers* associated with overhead activities. Activity-based costing is useful for analyzing the often complex processes of manufacturing or service delivery.

INVENTORY TURNOVER

In earlier parts, we described ratios and percentages that are useful in analyzing financial statements. For example, the gross margin percentage is a ratio of

$$\frac{\text{Gross margin}}{\text{Sales revenue}}$$

A useful ratio for analyzing inventory is the **inventory turnover ratio.** This ratio shows how many *times* the inventory turned over during a year. It is found by dividing Cost of Sales for a period by Inventory at the end of the period (or by the average inventory during the period).

Example. Cost of sales for 2005 was $1,000,000. Inventory on December 31, 2005, was $200,000. The inventory turnover ratio, showing how many times the inventory turned over in 2005, was

$$\frac{\text{Cost of sales}}{\text{Inventory}} = \frac{\$1,000,000}{\$200,000} = 5 \text{ times}$$

Slow-moving inventory ties up capital and increases the risk that the goods will become obsolete. Thus, an inventory turnover of five times is generally better than an inventory turnover of four times. However, if inventory is too small, orders from customers may not be filled promptly, which can result in lost sales revenue. This would reduce both cash and income.

Look back at the calculation of the inventory turnover ratio. The turnover ratio can be increased either by selling more goods with the same level of inventory or by having less inventory for the same amount of sales volume.

KEY POINTS TO REMEMBER

- If an entity has no record of the cost of the specific items that were sold during a period, it deduces cost of sales by (1) adding purchases to the beginning inventory, which gives the goods available for sale, and (2) subtracting the cost of the ending inventory. In doing this, the entity must make an assumption as to which items were sold.

- The first-in, first-out (FIFO) method assumes that the oldest items are the first to be sold.

- The last-in, first-out (LIFO) method assumes that the most recently purchased items are the first to be sold. In periods of rising prices, it results in a higher Cost of Sales and hence a lower taxable income than the FIFO method.

- The average-cost method charges both Cost of Sales and the ending Inventory at the average cost of the goods available for sale.

- The inventory method that a company selects **does not necessarily reflect the physical flow of its goods.**

- If the fair value (i.e., market value) of items in inventory decreases below their cost, the inventory is written down to fair value.

- The cost of goods produced in a manufacturing company is the sum of their direct materials cost, direct labor cost, and production overhead cost.

- Period costs are costs that are charged as expenses in the period in which the costs were incurred. Product costs become Cost of Sales in the period in which the products are sold, which may be later than the period in which the products were manufactured.

- Overhead is charged to products by means of an overhead rate, such as a rate per direct labor dollar.

- The inventory turnover ratio shows how many times the inventory turned over during a year.

PART 7

Noncurrent Assets and Depreciation

This part describes
- How plant assets are recorded in the accounts
- The meaning and significance of straight-line and accelerated depreciation
- How depreciation is recorded
- The meaning of depletion and how it is recorded
- How intangible assets are recorded

NONCURRENT ASSETS

Earlier, you learned that current assets are cash or items likely to be converted to cash within one year. Evidently, **noncurrent assets** are expected to be of use to the entity for longer than one year.

Tangible assets are assets than can be touched. Tangible assets include things like inventory, land, and buildings. **Intangible assets** are assets that have no physical substance (other than pieces of paper) but give the entity valuable rights. Some intangible assets are prepaid expenses, notes payable, and goodwill.

On the balance sheet, tangible noncurrent assets are often labeled **fixed assets** or **property, plant,** and **equipment.** Equipment is a noncurrent, tangible asset. For brevity, we shall use the word "plant" for all tangible noncurrent assets except land. Thus, buildings, equipment, and furniture are items of plant. These assets are expected to be useful for longer than one year.

ACCOUNTING FOR ACQUISITIONS

When an item of plant is acquired, it is recorded in the accounts at its cost in accordance with the fundamental accounting concept known as the **asset-measurement concept.** This is because it is a nonmonetary asset.

The cost of an asset includes all costs incurred to make the asset ready for its intended use.

> *Example.* Bird Corporation paid $50,000 for a plot of land. It also paid $1,500 as a brokers' fee, $600 for legal fees, and $5,000 to tear down the existing structures in order to make the land ready for a new building. The land should be recorded in the accounts at an amount of $57,100. (Some accountants charge the $5,000 as a cost of the new building.)

Transportation and installation costs are usually included as part of equipment cost. For example, assume that Plymouth Bank purchased a computer for $40,000. The bank also paid $200 in freight charges and $2,000 in installation charges. This equipment should be recorded in the accounts at its cost, $41,200.

If an entity constructs a machine or a building with its own personnel, all costs incurred in construction are included in the asset amount.

> *Example.* Thayer Company built a new building for its own use. It spent $400,000 in materials, $1,600,000 in salaries to workers directly engaged in the building's construction, and $600,000 to purchase services and $300,000 in overhead costs related to the building. This building should be recorded in the accounts at its cost, $2,900,000 (= $400,000 + $1,600,000 + $600,000 + $300,000).

CAPITAL LEASES

Most assets are *owned* by the entity. When an entity **leases** (i.e., rents) a building, a machine, or another tangible item, the item is owned by someone else (the **lessor**); the entity does not own it. In other words, most leased items are not assets of the entity that leases them (the **lessee**).

However, if an entity leases an item for a long period of time, it has as much control over the use of that item as if it owned it. A lease for a long time—almost the whole life of the asset—is called a **capital lease.** Because the entity controls the item for almost its whole life, a capital lease is recorded as an asset.

The amount recorded for a capital lease is the amount the entity would have paid if it had purchased the item rather than leased it. If an entity leased a machine for 10 years, agreeing to pay $10,000 per year, and if the purchase price of this machine was $70,000, the capital lease would be recorded at an amount of $70,000, as in this entry:

```
Dr. Capital Lease...........70,000
    Cr. Lease Obligation .....          70,000
```

Even though the entity does not own the item, a capital lease is treated like other plant assets. A capital lease is an exception to the general rule that assets are property or property rights that are owned by the entity. Special rules apply to accounting for capital leases. They are beyond the scope of this introductory treatment.

DEPRECIATION

Except in rare cases, land retains its usefulness indefinitely. Land therefore continues to be reported on the balance sheet at its acquisition cost, in accordance with the asset-measurement concept. This is because land is a nonmonetary asset. If Hanover Hospital purchased a plot of land in 1990 at a cost of $100,000, it would have been reported at $100,000 on the December 31, 1990, balance sheet. If Hanover Hospital still owned the land in 2006, and its market value then was $300,000, it would be reported on the December 31, 2006, balance sheet at $100,000.

Unlike land, plant assets eventually become useless. They have a limited life. Plant assets will become completely useless at some future time. At that time, the item is no longer an asset. Usually, this process occurs gradually; that is, a portion of the asset is used up in each year of its life, until finally it is scrapped or sold and therefore is no longer useful to the entity. At that time, it is not an asset.

The period of time over which a plant asset is estimated to be of service to the company is called its **service life.** When a machine or another item of plant is acquired, we do not know how long it actually will be of service. Therefore, we must estimate its service life.

Since some portion of a plant asset is used up during each year of its service life, a portion of the cost of the asset is treated as an expense in each year. For example, suppose a machine is purchased at a cost of $50,000. It has an estimated service life of five years and will be worthless then. It would be reasonable to charge one-fifth, or $10,000, as expense in each of the five years.

The portion of the cost of a plant asset that is recognized as an expense during each year of its estimated service life is called **depreciation.** The $10,000 recorded as an expense during each one of the five years of service life of the machine that cost $50,000 is called the depreciation expense for that year.

A plant asset can become useless for either of two reasons: (1) it may wear out physically or (2) it may become obsolete (i.e., no longer useful). The latter reason is called **obsolescence.** Loss of usefulness because of the development of improved equipment, changes in style, and other causes not related to the physical condition of the asset are examples of obsolescence.

The **service life** of an asset considers both physical wear and obsolescence. The service life is the shorter of the two periods. Thus, an asset with an estimated physical life of 10 years that is estimated to become obsolete in 5 years has an estimated service life of 5 years.

Since depreciation considers obsolescence, it is not correct to regard depreciation and obsolescence as two different things.

To summarize,

- Depreciation is the process of converting the cost of an asset into expense over its service life.

- This process recognizes that an asset gradually loses its usefulness.

- An asset can lose its usefulness for either of two reasons: (1) it wears out or (2) it becomes obsolete.

- The asset's service life is the shorter of these two causes.

In the preceding summary, no mention was made of market value. Depreciation is not related to changes in the market value of an asset. This is consistent with the asset-measurement concept.

In some cases, an entity expects to be able to sell the plant asset at the end of its service life. The amount that it expects to sell it for is called its **residual value.** If an entity buys a truck for $60,000 and expects to sell it for $10,000 five years later, the estimated residual value is $10,000. In most cases, an entity expects that a plant asset will be worthless at the end of its service life. If so, its residual value is zero.

Note that the residual value, as such, does not appear in the accounts. It is merely an estimated number used to calculate depreciation.

Example. Suppose a restaurant oven that cost $22,000 is expected to have a residual value of $2,000 at the end of its 10-year life. In this case, the total amount of depreciation that should be recorded during the service life of the asset is only $20,000. The depreciation expense for each of the 10 years would be $2,000 (= $20,000 × 1/10).

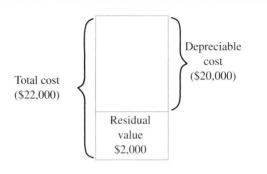

The difference between the cost of a plant asset and its residual value is called the **depreciable cost.** Thus, if an automobile purchased for $30,000 is expected to have a five-year life and to have a residual value of $5,000 at the end of that life, $30,000 is the cost and $25,000 is the depreciable cost.

Following is a list of factors that are relevant to the depreciation of an asset:

1. Original cost
2. Residual value
3. Service life

We use factors 1 and 2 to arrive at depreciable cost. All three factors are used to calculate depreciation expense for a given year. Note that factors 2 and 3 are estimates.

DEPRECIATION METHODS

There are many methods of calculating the cost that is to be recorded as depreciation expense in each year of the estimated service life. In the following sections, we describe three of them:

1. Units-of-production depreciation
2. Straight-line depreciation
3. Accelerated depreciation

Units-of-Production Depreciation

In the **units-of-production method,** a cost per unit of production is calculated, and depreciation expense for a year is found by multiplying this unit cost by the number of units that the asset produced in that year.

Example. Grady Company purchased a truck in 2005 for $44,000. It estimated that the truck would provide services for 100,000 miles and would have a residual value of $4,000.

Its depreciable cost was $40,000 (= $44,000 − $4,000).

Its estimated cost per mile was $0.40 (= $40,000/ 100,000 miles).

In 2006, the truck was driven 15,000 miles. Its depreciation expense in 2006 was $6,000 (= $0.40 × 15,000 miles).

Straight-Line Depreciation

The depreciation of a plant asset with a cost of $10,000, no residual value, and a five-year life may be graphed as follows:

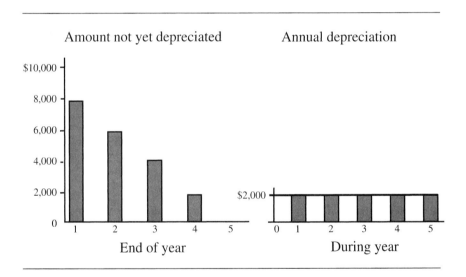

The line showing depreciation expense as a function of time is a straight line. Because of this, charging off an equal fraction of the asset cost each year is called the **straight-line method** of depreciation. Most companies use this method.

The percentage of cost charged off each year is called the **depreciation rate.** In the straight-line method, we obtain the rate by finding:

$$\frac{1}{\text{number of years of service life}}$$

Examples.

If the estimated life of an asset is:	The straight-line depreciation rate is:
2 years	50 %
3 years	33-1/3 %
4 years	25 %
5 years	20 %

In the straight-line method, the amount of depreciation expense for a given year is found by multiplying the depreciable cost by the depreciation rate. Thus, if the depreciable cost is $9,000 and the depreciation rate is 20%, the amount of depreciation expense each year will be $1,800.

Accelerated Depreciation

If you want an automobile to go faster, you press down on the accelerator. **Accelerated Depreciation** writes off the cost of an asset faster than straight-line depreciation. In accelerated depreciation, more depreciation expense is reported in the early years of the asset's service life and therefore less in the later years. The total amount of depreciation expense is the same as in the straight-line method.

There are many ways of calculating accelerated depreciation amounts. The following table shows one of them. The asset has a depreciable cost of $15,000 and a service life of five years.

Year	Accelerated Depreciation	Straight-line Depreciation	Accelerated is
1	$5,000	$3,000	larger
2	4,000	3,000	larger
3	3,000	3,000	same
4	2,000	3,000	smaller
5	1,000	3,000	smaller
Total	15,000	15,000	same

Accelerated depreciation is used principally in calculating taxable income. Taxable income and accounting income are not always the same; hence, the income tax paid and the income tax expense may be different. The difference becomes a liability account on the balance sheet called Deferred Income Taxes. This concept is beyond the introductory material in this text.

ACCOUNTING FOR DEPRECIATION

In Part 5, we described how certain types of assets are converted into expenses with the passage of time. When this occurs, there is a Cr. entry to the asset account, which shows the decrease in the amount of the asset, and there is an equal Dr. to the expense account.

> *Example.* If an entity had a fuel oil asset of $2,000 at the beginning of March and used $500 of fuel oil during March, the entity would recognize $500 of fuel oil expense for March and an equal decrease of $500 in the fuel oil asset. On the balance sheet of March 31, the fuel oil asset would be reported at $1,500 ($2,000 − $500).

In accounting for depreciation, the procedure is similar. First, we recognize the appropriate amount of expense for the period. In this case, the title of the expense account is Depreciation Expense.

Next, we must recognize an equal decrease in the amount of the asset. However, accountants prefer to show the original cost of plant assets on the balance sheet at all times. Therefore, decreases in the amount of a plant asset are not shown as a direct reduction in the asset amount. Instead, decreases in the asset amount of a plant asset because of depreciation expense are accumulated in a separate account called **Accumulated Depreciation.**

A decrease in an asset is always a credit. Accumulated Depreciation is a decrease in an asset and therefore has a Cr. balance. (Accumulated Depreciation is called a *contra-asset* account.)

If $1,000 of depreciation expense is recognized for a given year, the appropriate journal entry would be

```
Dr. Depreciation Expense .........1,000
    Cr. Accumulated Depreciation ..    1,000
```

On the balance sheet, the balance in the Accumulated Depreciation account is shown as a deduction from the original cost of the asset, and the remaining amount is called **Book Value.** For example, the listing

Plant	$10,000
Less accumulated depreciation	4,000
Book value	$ 6,000

shows that the plant originally cost $10,000, that $4,000 of its original cost has so far been recognized as depreciation expense, and that $6,000 of book value remains to be depreciated in future years. (Part of the book value may be the estimated residual value.)

If the depreciation expense on this machine was $1,000 per year, we know that depreciation expense has been taken for four years and that it will be taken for six more years in the future, assuming zero residual value. Each year, the write-off of $1,000 of the cost of the asset would be recorded with the following journal entry:

```
Dr. Depreciation Expense .........1,000
    Cr. Accumulated Depreciation ..    1,000
```

The following table shows the original cost, annual depreciation expense, accumulated depreciation (at year-end), and book value (at year-end) for a plant asset with an original cost of $5,000, a service life of five years, and zero residual value.

Year	Original Cost	Depreciation Expense	Accumulated Depreciation	Book Value
2005	$5,000	$1,000	$1,000	$4,000
2006	5,000	1,000	2,000	3,000
2007	5,000	1,000	3,000	2,000
2008	5,000	1,000	4,000	1,000
2009	5,000	1,000	5,000	0

The total amount charged as depreciation expense during the service life of the asset is thus $5,000.

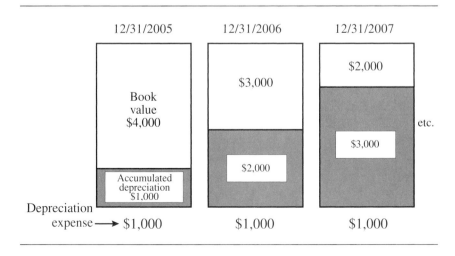

At the end of 2007, for example, the asset would be reported on the company's balance sheet as

Plant	$5,000
Less accumulated depreciation	3,000
Book value	$2,000

After the cost of an asset has been completely written off as depreciation expense, no more depreciation is recorded, even though the asset continues to be used. In the preceding example, the book value at the end of 2009 is zero. If the asset continued to be used in 2010, depreciation expense in 2010 would be zero.

To calculate the book value of an asset, you must subtract the accumulated depreciation from the original cost. Book value does not report the fair value of the asset.

Sale of a Plant Asset

The calculation of book value depends on estimates of service life and residual value. Because the actual residual value probably differs from these estimates, the amount realized from the sale of a plant asset will probably be different from its book value.

The difference between book value and the amount actually realized from a sale of a plant asset is called a **gain** (or **loss**) **on disposition of plant.** For example, if an asset whose book value is $10,000 is sold for $12,000, $2,000 is the gain on disposition of plant and is so reported on the income statement.

When the asset is sold, its cost and accumulated depreciation are removed from the accounts. For an asset that cost $40,000, had accumulated depreciation of $30,000, and sold for $12,000, the journal entry would be:

```
Cash ............................12,000
Accumulated depreciation .........30,000
   Plant ........................     40,000
   Gain on disposition of plant ...      2,000
```

Note that the above journal entry removes any trace of the assets from the balance sheet and records the amount greater than the book value as a gain.

Significance of Depreciation

The purpose of depreciation is to write off a fair share of the cost of the asset in each year in which it provides service. Actually, an asset may be as valuable at the end of a year as at the beginning. Depreciation expense for a given year does not represent a decrease in the asset's real value or usefulness during the year.

Remember that, in accounting for a plant asset, original cost is known; service life and residual value are both estimates.

The book value of a plant asset represents that portion of the cost not yet expensed. Therefore, the statement "book value reports what the asset is worth" is incorrect.

DEPLETION

Natural resources, such as coal, oil, and other minerals, are called **wasting assets.**

When the supply of oil in a well or coal in a mine is reduced, the asset is said to be depleted. **Depletion** is the name for the process of writing off the cost of these wasting assets. The depletion of a wasting asset is similar to the depreciation of a plant asset. However, in accounting for depletion, the asset account is reduced directly. Therefore, an accumulated depletion account is not ordinarily used.

Depletion is usually calculated by multiplying the quantity of the resource used in a period by a unit cost.

> ***Example.*** In 2005, Cecil Company purchased a coal mine for $3,000,000 and estimated that the mine contained 1,000,000 tons of coal, it would use a unit cost of $3 per ton.

In 2006, Cecil Company mined 100,000 tons of coal. The cost of this coal was estimated to be $3 per ton. The depletion expense in 2006 was $300,000. The coal mine would appear on the balance sheet for December 31, 2006, as

```
Coal mine .....$2,700,000
```

INTANGIBLE ASSETS

In accordance with the asset-measurement concept, intangible items, such as goodwill, trademarks, and patents, are not treated as assets unless they have been acquired at a measurable cost.

When intangibles are recognized as assets, their cost is written off over their service life. For example, patents have a maximum life of 17 years. In no case can the life of an intangible asset exceed 40 years. The process of writing off the cost of intangible assets is called **amortization.**

In summary, three terms that refer to writing off an asset's costs are

1. **Depreciation,**which refers to *plant* assets
2. **Depletion,**which refers to *wasting* assets
3. **Amortization,**which refers to *intangible* assets

The accounting treatment of a trademark is similar to that of goodwill. If Company A reports $1,000,000 of trademarks on its balance sheet, but Company B reports no such item, it is most likely that Company A has purchased trademarks but Company B has not.

Although we have used the word "amortization" just for intangible assets, amortization is sometimes used as a general term for expensing the cost of all assets; that is, some people call depreciation and depletion special cases of amortization.

KEY POINTS TO REMEMBER

- When acquired, a plant asset is recorded at its cost, including installation and other costs of making the asset ready for its intended use.

- Land has an unlimited life and is rarely depreciated.

- Plant assets are depreciated over their service life. Each year, a fraction of their cost is debited to Depreciation Expense and credited to Accumulated Depreciation.

- Depreciation Expense is an estimate. We do not know how long the service life will be or the asset's residual value.

- The book value of a plant asset is the difference between its cost and its accumulated depreciation. When book value reaches zero or the residual value, no more depreciation expense is recorded.

- Book value does *not* report what the asset is worth.

- When an asset is sold, the difference between the sale price and book value is a gain or loss and is so reported on the income statement.

- In financial accounting, depreciation is calculated either by an accelerated method or by the straight-line method.

- In the units-of-production method, the annual depreciation expense is calculated by multiplying the number of service units produced in that year by a unit cost. This unit cost is found by dividing the asset's depreciable cost by the number of service units estimated to be produced over the asset's total life.

- In the straight-line method, the annual depreciation expense is calculated by multiplying the asset's depreciable cost by a constant percentage. This percentage is found by dividing 1 by the number of years in the asset's estimated service life.

- Accelerated depreciation is often used for income tax purposes because it decreases the amount of taxable income in the early years.

- Taxable income may differ from pretax income reported on the income statement. If so, the difference between the tax expense and the amount of tax actually paid is a balance sheet item, Deferred Income Taxes.

- Depletion is the process of writing off wasting assets, and amortization is the process of writing off intangible assets. The accounting for both processes is similar to depreciation, except that the credit is made directly to the asset account.

PART 8

Liabilities and Equity

This part describes
* The nature of working capital
* Types of permanent capital: debt and equity
* How to account for debt capital
* Accounting for equity capital in proprietorships, partnerships, and corporations
* Paid-in capital: common and preferred stock
* Retained earnings and dividends
* The debt/equity ratio
* The nature of consolidated financial statements

WORKING CAPITAL

The balance sheet has two sides with equal totals:

LOUGEE COMPANY
Balance Sheet as of December 31, 2005

Assets		Liabilities and Equity	
Current assets	$10,000	Current liabilities	$4,000
Noncurrent assets	20,000	Noncurrent liabilities	9,000
		Paid-in capital	7,000
		Retained earnings	10,000
Total assets	$30,000	Total liabilities and equity	$30,000

Current assets are assets that are expected to be turned into cash within one year. Current liabilities are obligations that come due within one year. For Lougee Company, we can say that $4,000 of the $10,000 in current assets was financed by the current liabilities. The remaining $6,000 of current assets and the $20,000 of noncurrent assets were financed by the $9,000 of noncurrent liabilities plus the $17,000 of equity.

That part of the current assets not financed by the current liabilities is called **working capital.** Working capital is therefore the difference between current assets and current liabilities. In the case of Lougee Company, working capital is

$$\$10,000 - \$4,000 = \$6,000$$

SOURCES OF CAPITAL

To highlight how working capital and the noncurrent assets were financed, we can rearrange the items on the balance sheet as follows:

LOUGEE COMPANY

Sources and Uses of Permanent Capital
as of December 31, 2005

Uses of Capital		Sources of Capital	
Working capital	$ 6,000	Noncurrent liabilities................	$ 9,000
Noncurrent assets	20,000	Equity	17,000
Total uses	$26,000	Total sources	$26,000

The right-hand side of the preceding balance sheet shows the sources of capital used to finance the working capital and the noncurrent assets. Collectively, these sources are called **permanent capital.** As the balance sheet indicates, there are two sources of permanent capital: (1) Noncurrent liabilities and (2) Equity. The total of these two sources is $26,000, and they are used to finance assets that also total $26,000.

In this part, we describe the two types of permanent capital and how they are recorded in the accounts. Although these items are called "capital," they are more accurately labeled "sources of capital."

USES   SOURCES

DEBT CAPITAL

Although most liabilities are debts, the term **debt capital** refers only to noncurrent liabilities. Debt capital therefore refers to liabilities that come due sometime after one year.

A common source of debt capital is the issuance of **bonds.** A bond is a written promise to pay someone who lends money to the entity. Since a bond usually is a noncurrent liability, the payments are due some time after one year. The total amount that must be repaid is specified on the face of a bond and is termed the face **amount.** If Green Company issues 10-year bonds whose face amounts total $100,000, Green Company has a liability, Bonds Payable, of $100,000. (If the entity does not receive cash equal to the face amount of the bonds, there are accounting complications not discussed in this book.)

> *Example.* Suppose that Green Company receives $100,000 cash from the issuance of bonds that have a face amount of $100,000. The journal entry necessary to record the effect of this transaction on the Cash and Bonds Payable accounts follows:

```
Dr. Cash ...................100,000
    Cr. Bonds Payable ......           100,000
```

When they are issued, bonds are noncurrent liabilities. However, as time passes and the due date becomes less than one year, a bond becomes a current liability. In 2005, a bond that is due on January 1, 2007, is a noncurrent liability. In 2006, the same bond is a current liability.

When an entity issues bonds, it assumes two obligations. It is obligated (1) to repay the face amount, the **principal,** on the due date and (2) to pay **interest,** often, but not always, at semiannual intervals (i.e., twice a year). The obligation to pay the principal is usually a noncurrent liability. The liability for interest that has been earned but is unpaid is a current liability.

Interest on bonds is an expense and should be recognized in the accounting period to which the interest applies.

> **Example.** If, in January 2006, an entity makes a semiannual interest payment of $3,000 to cover the last six months of 2005, this interest expense should be recognized in 2005. This is required by the matching concept.
>
> The $3,000 of unpaid interest that was an expense in 2005 is recorded in 2005 by the following entry:
>
> ```
> Dr. Interest Expense.......3,000
>    Cr. Interest Payable ...          3,000
> ```
>
> In 2006, when this interest was paid to the bondholders, the following entry would be made:
>
> ```
> Dr. Interest Payable.......3,000
>    Cr. Cash ..............            3,000
> ```
>
> As these entries indicate, the liability for the principal payment is the total face value of the bond, but the interest liability is the amount of interest expense incurred but unpaid.

Some companies obtain funds by issuing an instrument that is backed by other instruments. For example, a bank may issue an instrument that promises to pay interest from a portfolio of mortgages it holds. The return on such an instrument is derived from the underlying mortgages, and the instrument is therefore called a **derivative.** Derivatives may be backed by a complicated set of promises. Therefore, measuring the value of a derivative and accounting for this value may be extremely complicated. Accounting for derivatives is described in advanced texts.

TYPES OF EQUITY CAPITAL

Unlike a bond, which is a promise to pay and therefore is a liability, equity is an ownership interest in the entity, and the entity does not promise to pay equity investors anything. Equity is not a liability. As noted in earlier parts, there are two sources of **equity capital:**

1. Amounts paid in by equity investors, who are the entity's owners; this amount is called Paid-in Capital
2. Amounts generated by the profitable operation of the entity; this amount is called Retained Earnings

Some entities do not report these two sources separately. An unincorporated business owned by a single person is called a **proprietorship.** The equity item in a proprietorship is often reported by giving the proprietor's name, followed by the word "Capital."

> *Example.* Mary Green is the proprietor of Green's Market. Green's Market has total equity of $10,000. The owner's equity item would appear as
>
> Mary Green, Capital $10,000

A **partnership** is an unincorporated business owned by two or more persons jointly. If there are only a few partners, the equity of each would be shown separately.

> *Example.* John Black and Henry Brown are equal partners in a laundry business. On December 31, 2005, the equity in the business totaled $100,000. The equity might be reported on that date as follows:
>
> | | |
> |---|---|
> | John Black, Capital | $ 50,000 |
> | Henry Brown, Capital | 50,000 |
> | Total equity | $100,000 |

Equity in a partnership consists of capital paid-in by owners, plus earnings retained in the business. Thus, the item "John Black, Capital, $50,000" means John Black's ownership interest in the assets is $50,000, including the capital he paid in plus his share of retained earnings.

Owners of a **corporation** are called **shareholders** (or stockholders) because they hold shares of the corporation's stock. The equity section of a corporation's balance sheet is therefore labeled shareholder equity.

There are two types of shareholders: **common shareholders** and **preferred shareholders.** The stock held by the former is called common stock, and that held by the latter is called preferred stock. We shall first describe accounting for common stock.

Most organizations are proprietorships, partnerships, or corporations. Other forms, not described here, include limited partnerships, trusts, and S Corporations. Special rules apply to equity transactions and/or tax accounting in these organizations.

Common Stock

Some stock is issued with a specific amount printed on the face of each certificate. This amount is called the **par value.** Strangely, the par value of stock has practically no significance. It is a holdover from the days when shareholders were liable if they purchased stock for less than its par value. In order to avoid this liability, stock today is always issued for much more than its par value. Nevertheless, the par value of stock continues to be reported on the balance sheet.

The amount that the shareholders paid the corporation in exchange for their stock is **paid-in capital.** The difference between par value and the total paid-in capital is called **additional paid-in capital.**

> *Example.* Jones paid $10,000 cash to Marple Company and received 1,000 shares of its $1 par-value common stock. Marple Company would make the following journal entry for this transaction:

```
Dr. Cash ..................10,000
    Cr. Common stock .......        1,000
    Cr. Additional paid-in capital  9,000
```

If Jones's payment of $10,000 were the only equity transaction, this section of the Marple Company balance sheet would appear as follows:

Common stock	$ 1,000
Additional paid-in capital	9,000
Total paid-in capital	$10,000

Not all stocks have a par value. For these **no-par-value stocks,** the directors state a value. This value, called the **stated value,** is usually set close to the amount that the corporation actually receives from the issuance of the stock. The difference between this amount and cash received is Additional Paid-in Capital, just as in the case of par-value stock.

When a corporation is formed, its directors vote to **authorize** a certain number of shares of stock and generally to **issue** some of this authorized stock to investors. Thus, at any given time, the amount of stock authorized is usually larger than the amount issued.

A corporation may buy back some of the stock that it had previously issued. Such stock is called **treasury stock.** The **outstanding stock** consists of the issued stock less the treasury stock. If a company issues 100,000 shares and buys back 15,000 shares, its treasury stock is 15,000 shares, and its outstanding stock is 85,000 shares.

The balance sheet amount for common stock is the amount for the number of shares of stock outstanding.

Example. Maxim Company has authorized 100,000 shares of stock. It has issued 60,000 shares, for which it received the stated value of $10 per share. As of December 31, 2005, it has bought back 10,000 shares, paying $10 per share. These shares are its treasury stock. The balance sheet amount for common stock is $500,000 [(60,000 × $10) − (10,000 × $10)].

Shareholders may sell their stock to other investors. Such sales do not affect the balance sheet of the corporation. This is an example of the entity concept.

When shareholders sell their stock to other investors, the price at which the sale takes place is determined in the **marketplace.** The value at which a stock is sold in such a transaction is called the **market value.** The market value of a company's stock has no necessary relation to its par value, its stated value, or the amount of paid-in capital. If the par value of a certain stock is $1, the market value can be any value. If the stated value of another stock is $10, the market value can be any value. If paid-in capital is $12 per share, the market value can be any value.

The amount reported as total equity equals total assets less total liabilities. On the balance sheet, this is not likely to equal the total market value of all stock outstanding. Accounting does not report the market value of the shareholders' equity.

Preferred Stock

Some corporations issue stock that gives its owners preferential treatment over the common shareholders. As the word "preferential" suggests, such stock is called **preferred stock.**

Usually, preferred shareholders have a preferential claim over the common shareholders for the par value of their stock. Thus, if the corporation were liquidated, the owner of 500 shares of $100 preferred stock would have to receive $50,000 before the common shareholders received anything.

As you learned earlier, par value of common stock has practically no significance. Because preferred stock usually does have a preferential claim on assets equal to its par value, its par value has some significance.

Preferred shareholders usually have rights to a stated amount of dividends. If Scott Corporation has issued $100,000 of 9% preferred stock, no dividend can be paid to common shareholders until the preferred shareholders have received their full dividend of 9% of $100,000, amounting to $9,000 per year.

RETAINED EARNINGS AND DIVIDENDS

The net income of a period increases equity. The directors may vote to distribute money to the shareholders in the form of **dividends.** Dividends decrease equity.

"Earnings" is another name for "net income." If earnings are not distributed as dividends, they are **retained** in the corporation. This amount is reported on the balance sheet as **Retained Earnings.** The Retained Earnings account increases by the amount of net income each period and decreases by the amount of dividends. Thus, if Retained Earnings is $100,000 at the start of a period during which a dividend of $20,000 is declared and during which net income is $30,000, Retained Earnings will be $110,000 at the end of the period.

Net income refers to the increase in equity in one year, whereas **retained earnings** refers to the net increases, after deduction of dividends, over the life of the corporation to date.

Retained earnings is one **source** of capital. It is reported on the right side of the balance sheet. The capital is in the form of assets, and assets are reported on the left side of the balance sheet. Some people think that retained earnings are assets. Retained earnings are *not* assets. Remember that Cash is an asset. Therefore, retained earnings *are not* cash.

Equity is sometimes called "net worth." This term suggests that the amount of equity shows what the owners' claim on the assets is *worth.* Because the amounts reported on the assets side of the balance sheet do not represent the real worth of these assets, this suggestion is wrong. The actual *worth* of a company's stock is what people will pay for it. This is the market price of the stock, which does not appear anywhere on the balance sheet.

DISTRIBUTIONS TO SHAREHOLDERS

Most corporations make an annual cash payment to their common shareholders. This is called a **dividend.** If Crowley Company declared and paid a dividend of $5 per share, and if it had 100,000 shares of common stock outstanding, the dividend would be $500,000. The journal entry to record the effect of this distribution on Cash and Retained Earnings would be

```
Dr. Retained Earnings.......500,000
    Cr. Cash ................        500,000
```

A company may distribute to shareholders a noncash asset, such as shares of stock in other companies it owns, or even one of its products. The effect of this distribution is a debit to Retained Earnings and an equal credit to the asset account.

Crowley Company might declare a **stock dividend.** If it distributed one share of its own stock for each 10 shares of stock outstanding, shareholders would have more shares. No asset decreased, so, in order to maintain equality, Equity would be unchanged.

Similarly, Crowley might send its shareholders additional shares equal to the number of shares they own or even double or triple this number of shares. Crowley may do this because it believes a high market price per share has an undesirable influence in trading the stock. This is called a **stock split.** If Crowley's stock previously had a market price of $200 per share for its 100,000 shares, and it made a "two-for-one" stock split, the number of shares of stock outstanding would increase. Cash would not change. The market price per share would decrease. A stock split has the same effect as a stock dividend. Cash is unchanged. Retained Earnings is unchanged. The market price per share decreases.

Although arithmetically a two-for-one stock split cuts the market price in half, in practice the decrease might be slightly less than this. The reason is that stocks with moderate stock prices tend to be regarded more favorably by investors than stocks with very high prices. This is generally the principal reason for making a stock split.

	Total amount of equity	Total number of shares outstanding
Cash dividend	decreases	unchanged
Stock dividend	unchanged	increases
Stock split	unchanged	increases

BALANCE BETWEEN DEBT AND EQUITY CAPITAL

A corporation obtains some capital from retained earnings. In addition, it obtains capital from the issuance of stock, which is equity capital, and from the issuance of bonds, which is debt capital.

A corporation has no fixed obligations to its common shareholders; that is, the company need not declare dividends each year and need not repay the amount the shareholders have invested.

A company has two fixed obligations to its bondholders, however:

• Payment of interest
• Repayment of principal

If the company fails to pay either the interest or the principal when due, the bondholders may force the company into bankruptcy. Bonds are a more risky method of raising capital by the corporation than stock; that is, debt capital is a more risky source of capital than equity capital.

Bonds are an obligation of the company that issues them, but stocks are not an obligation. Therefore, *investors* usually have more risk if they invest in a company's stock than if they invest in the bonds of the same company. They are not certain to get either dividends or repayment of their investment. Investors therefore demand a higher return from an investment in stock than from an investment in bonds in the same company. They are not sure of getting their dividends or repayment of their investment. Investors therefore expect a higher return from an investment in stock than from an investment in bonds in the same company. The trade-off between risk and return is a more advanced concept that is treated in most finance texts.

For example, if a company's bonds had an interest rate of 7%, investors would invest in its stock only if they expected that the return on stock would be considerably more than 7%. (The expected return on stock consists of both expected dividends and an expected increase in the market value of the stock.)

Thus, from the viewpoint of the issuing company, stock, which is equity capital, is a more expensive source of capital than bonds, which are debt capital.

The principal differences between debt capital and equity capital can be summarized as

	Bonds (Debt)	Stock (Equity)
Annual payments required	Yes	No
Principal payments required	Yes	No
Risk to the entity is	High	Low
But its cost is relatively	Low	High

In deciding on its permanent capital structure, a company must decide on the proper balance between debt capital, which has a relatively high risk and a relatively low cost, and equity capital, which has a relatively low risk and a relatively high cost.

A company runs the risk of going bankrupt if it has too high a proportion of debt capital. A company pays an unnecessarily high cost for its permanent capital if it has too high a proportion of equity capital.

A company that obtains a high proportion of its permanent capital from debt is said to be *highly leveraged*. If such a company does not get into financial difficulty, it will earn a high return for its equity investors, because each dollar of debt capital takes the place of a more expensive dollar of equity capital.

However, highly leveraged companies are risky because the high proportion of debt capital and the associated requirement to pay interest increases the chance that the company will not be able to meet its obligations.

In this introductory treatment, we focus on the basic difference between common stock and bonds. Some additional points are worth noting:

1. The interest on bonds is a tax-deductible expense to the corporation. If the annual interest expense on a 9% bond is $90,000, the corporation's taxable income is reduced by $90,000. At a tax rate of 40%, this means that the net cost to the corporation is only 60% of $90,000, or $54,000; the effective interest cost is 5.4%.

2. Preferred stock has risk and cost characteristics that are in between common stocks and bonds. Although dividends on preferred stock do not reduce a corporation's taxable income, many companies still use preferred stock as a source of capital.

3. In recent years, there has been a tremendous increase in the types of debt and equity securities. New financial instruments are structured with risk and cost characteristics designed to meet the needs of various types of investors.

DEBT RATIO

A common way of measuring the relative amount of debt and equity capital is the **debt ratio**, which is the ratio of **debt capital** to total permanent capital. Recall that "debt capital" is another name for noncurrent liabilities. Equity capital consists of total Paid-in Capital plus Retained Earnings.

Earlier, we worked with the following permanent capital structure:

LOUGEE COMPANY

Sources and Uses of Permanent Capital
as of December 31, 2005

Uses of Capital		Sources of Capital	
Working capital	$ 6,000	Noncurrent liabilities	$ 9,000
Noncurrent assets	20,000	Equity	17,000
Total uses	$26,000	Total sources	$26,000

The debt ratio for Lougee Company can be calculated as

$$\frac{\text{Debt capital (noncurrent liabilities)}}{\text{Debt capital} + \text{equity capital}} = \frac{\$9,000}{\$26,000} = 35\%$$

Most industrial companies have a debt ratio of less than 50%. Lougee Company is in this category.

CONSOLIDATED FINANCIAL STATEMENTS

If one corporation owns more than 50% of the stock in another corporation, it can control the affairs of that corporation because it can outvote all other owners. Many businesses consist of a number of corporations that are legally separate entities but, because they are controlled by one corporation, are part of a single "family." A corporation which controls one or more other corporations is called the **parent,** and the controlled corporations are called **subsidiaries.**

> ***Example.*** Palm Company owns 100% of the stock of Sea Company, 60% of the stock of Sand Company, and 40% of the stock of Gray Company. The parent company is Palm Company. The subsidiaries are Sea Company and Sand Company.

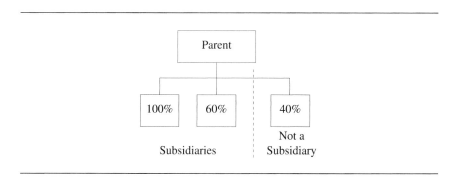

Since the management of the parent corporation, Palm Company, controls the activities of Sea Company and Sand Company, these three companies function as a single entity. The entity concept requires that a set of financial statements be prepared for this family.

Each corporation is a legal entity with its own financial statements. The set of financial statements for the whole family brings together, or **consolidates,** these separate statements. The set for the whole family is therefore called a **consolidated financial statement.**

For example, if Palm Company has $10,000 cash, Sea Company has $5,000 cash, and Sand Company has $4,000 cash, the whole family has $19,000 cash, and this amount would be reported on the consolidated balance sheet.

An entity earns income by making sales to outside customers. It cannot earn income by dealing with itself. Corporations in the consolidated family may buy from and sell to one another. Transactions between members of the family do not earn income for the consolidated entity. The effect of these **intrafamily transactions** therefore must be eliminated from the consolidated statements.

> *Example.* Palm Company had sales revenue of $1,000,000, Sea Company had sales revenue of $200,000, and Sand Company had sales revenue of $400,000. Palm Company sold $30,000 of products to Sea Company. All other sales were to outside customers. On the consolidated income statement, the amount of sales reported would be $1,570,000 (= $1,000,000 + $200,000 + $400,000 − $30,000 of intrafamily sales).

Intrafamily transactions are also eliminated from the consolidated balance sheet. For example, if Sand Company owed Palm Company $10,000, this amount would appear as Accounts Receivable on the balance sheet of Palm Company and as Accounts Payable on the balance sheet of Sand Company. On the consolidated balance sheet, the Accounts Receivable and Accounts Payable would each be $10,000 less than the sum of these amounts on the balance sheets of each of the family members.

The balance sheet of Palm Company reports as an asset the Sand Company and Sea Company stock that it owns. This asset must be eliminated from the consolidated balance sheet. On the balance sheets of the subsidiaries, the corresponding amounts are reported as equity, and these amounts are eliminated on the consolidated balance sheet.

> *Example.* Palm Company owns 60% of the stock of Sand Company. This stock was reported on the balance sheet of Palm Company as an asset, Investment in Subsidiaries, at $60,000. The total equity of Sand Corporation is $100,000. On the consolidated balance sheet, the $60,000 asset would be eliminated, and, because debits must equal credits, $60,000 of Sand Company's consolidated equity also would be eliminated.

Palm Company owns 40% of Gray Company stock. This asset is listed on Palm Company's balance sheet at $100,000. It would not be eliminated from the consolidated balance sheet, because only companies of which the parent owns more than 50% are consolidated.

Palm Company owns 60% of Sand Company's stock, which is a majority of the stock. Other shareholders own the other 40% of Sand Company stock; they are minority shareholders. They have an interest in the consolidated entity, and this interest is reported in the liabilities and equity side of the consolidated balance sheet. It is labeled **minority interest.**

The consolidated income statement reports revenues from sales to outside parties only and expenses resulting from costs incurred with outside parties. Intrafamily revenues and expenses are eliminated.

The consolidated financial statements report on the entity called "Palm Company and Subsidiaries." This family of corporations is an economic entity, but it is not a legal entity.

Many corporations have subsidiaries. Since the consolidated financial statements give the best information about the economic entity, many published financial statements are consolidated financial statements.

In an entity with dozens of subsidiaries, some of which have their own subsidiaries, eliminating the intrafamily transactions is a complicated task. Only the general principles have been described here.

KEY POINTS TO REMEMBER

- A company obtains its permanent capital from two sources: (1) debt (i.e., noncurrent liabilities) and (2) equity. It uses this capital to finance (1) working capital (i.e., current assets − current liabilities) and (2) noncurrent assets.

- Most debt capital is obtained by issuing bonds. Bonds obligate the company to pay interest and to repay the principal when it is due.

- Equity capital is obtained by (1) issuing shares of stock and (2) retaining earnings.

- The amount of capital obtained from preferred and common shareholders is the amount they paid in. The par, or stated, value of common stock is not an important number today, but it is still reported on the balance sheet.

- Cash dividends decrease the amount of equity capital. Stock dividends and stock splits do not affect the total equity.

- Retained earnings are total earnings (i.e., net income) since the entity began operations, less total dividends. (A net loss, of course, results in a decrease in retained earnings.)

- Although sometimes called "net worth," the amount of owners' equity does not show what the owners' interest is worth.

- In deciding on its permanent capital structure, a company attempts to strike the right balance between (1) risky but low-cost debt capital and (2) less risky but high-cost equity capital. For a given company, this balance is indicated by its debt ratio.

- Many companies have subsidiaries. The economic entity is a family consisting of a parent and its subsidiaries (in which, by definition, it owns more than 50% of the stock). Consolidated financial statements are prepared for such an economic entity by combining their separate financial statements and eliminating transactions among members of the family.

- The consolidated balance sheet reports all the assets owned by the consolidated entity and all the claims of parties outside the family.

- The consolidated income statement reports only revenues from sales to outside parties and expenses resulting from costs incurred with outside parties. Intrafamily revenues and expenses are eliminated.

PART 9

Statement of Cash Flows

This part describes
* What a statement of cash flows is
* How a statement of cash flows differs from an income statement
* The meaning of the term "cash flow from operations"
* The relationship of depreciation to cash flow
* The content of the other two sections on the statement of cash flows, investing and financing activites
* Uses of the statement of cash flows

A company must prepare three financial statements. We described two of them in earlier parts. The balance sheet reports the financial status of the company as of the end of each accounting period. The income statement reports financial performance during the period. In this part, we describe the third required statement. It reports the **flow of cash** during the accounting period, and it is therefore called the **statement of cash flows,** or cash flow statement.

Both the income statement and the cash flow statement report flows during the period. The difference is that the income statement reports flows on the **accrual** basis; that is, inflows are measured as revenues and outflows are measured as expenses. By contrast, the statement of cash flows reports inflows and outflows of cash. The income statement focuses on *profitability.* The statement of cash flows focuses on *liquidity* and *solvency.*

Example. Assume that an entity sold goods for $1,000 on May 1, and the customer paid $1,000 for these goods on June 1. Its cash inflow on May 1 would be $0, while its revenue in May would be $1,000. Its cash inflow on June 1 would be $1,000, and its revenue in June would be $0/$1,000. Its balance sheet at the end of May would include this $1,000 as an asset, called Accounts Receivable. Therefore, an entity's revenues and expenses in a period do not necessarily match its cash receipts and disbursements in that period. This is one of the most important concepts to understand in learning financial accounting.

There are two acceptable methods of preparing the statement of cash flows. One is to summarize the inflows and outflows to the Cash account directly; it is therefore called the **direct method.** Most companies, however, use the other method, which is called the **indirect method.**

Companies that use the indirect method report their cash flows *indirectly* by adjusting net income to remove the effects of accrual accounting. The indirect method is much more widely used because it shows the relationship between the income statement and the balance sheet and therefore aids in the analysis of these statements.

The indirect method uses balance sheet account changes to determine whether such changes had a positive or negative impact on cash flow. Since the balance sheet must always stay in balance, it is easy to determine the impact on cash by analyzing changes in each of the other accounts.

In preparing the statement of cash flows, we are interested in *changes* in the balance sheet accounts from one accounting period to another. The purpose of the statement of cash flows is to provide information about items that caused the change in cash from one balance sheet to another. This will help us to understand the *sources and uses of cash* during the accounting period.

In this part, we develop a statement of cash flows for Arlen Company, using the indirect method and the balance sheet and income statement information in Exhibit 9.1. This statement is given in Exhibit 9.2. The statement of cash flows in Exhibit 9.2 consists of three sections. We shall describe the first section, called "Cash Flow from Operating Activities," in some detail. We shall describe the other two sections, called "Cash Flow from Investing Activities" and "Cash Flow from Financing Activities," together because the same principles apply to both. The principal purpose of this part is to show the relationship between the accrual accounting numbers and cash.

Exhibit 9.1

ARLEN COMPANY

Balance Sheets ($000 Omitted)

Assets

	As of December 31			
	2006		**2005**	
Current assets				
Cash		$ 20		$ 7
Accounts receivable		40		42
Inventory		60		56
Prepaid expenses		20		20
Total current assets		140		125
Noncurrent assets				
Land		$30		$ 30
Plant, at cost	$120		$108	
Less accumulated depreciation	70	50	64	44
Goodwill and patents		10		10
Total assets		230		209

Liabilities and Equity

		2006		2005
Current liabilities				
Accounts payable		$ 30		$ 33
Accrued wages		10		6
Income taxes payable		20		20
Total current liabilities		60		59
Noncurrent liabilities				
Mortgage bonds payable		40		34
Total liabilities		100		93
Shareholder equity				
Paid-in capital (4,800 shares outstanding)		$ 60		$ 60
Retained earnings		70		56
Total shareholder equity		130		116
Total liabilities and equity		230		209

Income Statement, 2006 ($000 Omitted)

		Percentage
Sales revenue	$300	100.0
Less cost of sales	− 180	60.0
Gross margin	120	40.0
Less depreciation expense	− 6	2.0
Other expenses	− 72	24.0
Earnings before interest and taxes	42	14.0
Interest expense	− 5	1.7
Earnings before income taxes	37	12.3
Provision for income taxes	− 13	4.3
Net income	24	8.0
Less dividends	− 10	
Addition to equity	14	

Exhibit 9.2

ARLEN COMPANY

Statement of Cash Flows, 2006

Cash Flow from Operating Activities

Net income		$ 24
Adjustments:		
Depreciation expense	$ 6	
Changes in working capital accounts:		
Decrease in accounts receivable....................................	2	
Increase in inventory	(4)	
Decrease in accounts payable..	(3)	
Increase in accrued wages	4	
Change in working capital..	(1)	
Total adjustments to net income......................................		5
Total cash flow from operating activities		29
Cash Flow from Investing Activities		
Purchase of plant		(12)
Cash Flow from Financing Activities		
Issuance of long-term debt	6	
Dividends paid...	(10)	
Total cash flow from financing activities		(4)
Net increase in cash and cash equivalents.....................		$13

Note: Parentheses indicate decreases in cash.

CASH FLOW FROM OPERATING ACTIVITIES

The first section of the statement of cash flows reports how much cash was generated by the operating activities of the period—the day-to-day activities that bring in cash from customers and pay out cash to employees and suppliers. To do this, we must first analyze the balance sheet accounts that contain information about the day-to-day operating activities. We need to focus first on the balance sheet accounts that are concerned with operating activities. We will then convert this information from an accrual basis to a cash basis.

Net income is the difference between revenues and expenses. "Cash Flow from Operating Activities" is the difference between *operating* cash inflows and *operating* cash outflows. To find the amount of cash flow from operating activities, we must make two types of adjustments to net income: (1) for depreciation and other expenses that will not ever require an outflow of cash and (2) for changes in working capital accounts (accounts that are an integral part of daily operating activities).

Recall from an earlier part of the book that net income is added to beginning Retained Earnings to arrive at ending Retained Earnings. With no dividends, the change in the balance sheet account called Retained Earnings is simply the Net Income for the accounting period.

ADJUSTMENT FOR DEPRECIATION EXPENSE

According to its balance sheet (Exhibit 9.1), Arlen Company owned Plant, most of which it had acquired prior to the year 2006 at a cost of $108,000. The cash outflow for these assets occurred prior to 2006.

According to its income statement, Arlen Company had a Depreciation expense of $6,000 in 2006. Depreciation recognizes a portion of the cost of fixed assets. The cash outflow for the assets on hand at the beginning of 2006 occurred in earlier years; this Depreciation expense therefore was not a cash outflow in 2006.

Although Depreciation expense is subtracted from Revenue in arriving at Net Income, it is not a cash outflow. Net income is $6,000 less than it would have been with no Depreciation expense. Therefore, in Exhibit 9.2, Net income is adjusted to a cash basis by adding $6,000 to Net income.

Suppose that Arlen Company had decided to recognize a Depreciation expense of $10,000, rather than $6,000, in 2006, but made no other changes in the accounts. The cash flow from operating activities would then be the same as the amount reported in Exhibit 9.2. This would occur because, if Depreciation expense was $4,000 higher than the amount reported in Exhibit 9.2, Net income would be $4,000 lower than the amount reported. The $4,000 increase in Depreciation expense would offset exactly the $4,000 decrease in Net income. Cash flow would therefore be the same as the amount reported in Exhibit 9.2.

To reinforce this point, recall the journal entry that records Depreciation Expense:

```
Dr. Depreciation Expense
    Cr. Accumulated Depreciation
```

The Cash account was not changed by this entry. To repeat, the cash for fixed assets was paid out when the fixed assets were purchased (or when borrowings made in connection with such a purchase were paid back). Cash is not affected by the depreciation charge; to do so would be double counting.

Amortization of intangible assets, write-off losses, and other noncash expenses also are added to net income to convert net income to cash flow from operating activities.

Thus, depreciation *is not* **a source of cash.** (This is a common misconception, due to the role it plays on the statement of cash flows to adjust net income to a cash basis.)

ADJUSTMENTS FOR CHANGES IN WORKING CAPITAL ACCOUNTS

Cash, accounts receivable, inventory, and similar items that will be converted into cash in the near future are current assets. Accounts payable, wages payable, and similar obligations that are due in the near future are current liabilities. The difference between current assets and current liabilities is called **working capital.** Operating activities—such as making sales; purchasing materials for inventory; and incurring production, selling, and administrative expenses—are the principal causes of change in working capital items. We shall analyze the asset and liability categories separately.

Although cash is, of course, an item of working capital, we exclude it here when we adjust for changes in working capital accounts because we want to analyze the impact of such changes on cash.

ADJUSTMENTS FOR CHANGES IN CURRENT ASSETS
No Change in Balance

If all revenues in 2006 were from cash sales, cash inflows would be the same amount as revenues; that is, if sales revenues were $300,000, cash inflows would be $300,000. However, in most companies, some sales are made to credit customers. These sales are first reported as the current asset, Accounts Receivable. The company will receive cash later on, when customers pay their bills.

In Arlen Company, all sales were credit sales. If sales in 2006 were $300,000, Revenues would be $300,000, and Accounts Receivable would increase by $300,000 when these sales were made.

The journal entry summarizing the preceding transaction would be (omitting 000)

```
Dr. Accounts Receivable.....300
    Cr. Revenues .............        300
```

If, in 2006, Arlen Company received $300,000 cash from credit customers, Cash would increase and Accounts Receivable would decrease, as summarized in the following journal entry:

```
Dr. Cash...................300
    Cr. Accounts Receivable ..300
```

The preceding two entries have been posted to the accounts:

Cash		Accounts Receivable	
Beg. bal. 7		Beg. bal. 42	From customer 300
From customer 300		Sale 300	
End. bal. 307		End bal. 42	

Revenues	
	Sale 300

As these accounts show, when the balance in Accounts Receivable does not change, the increase in cash is the same as the sales revenue.

This is the case with all working capital accounts. If the beginning balance is the same as the ending balance, an adjustment from the accrual basis to the cash basis is not necessary when preparing the statement of cash flows.

Current Asset Balance Decreased

Now consider what the account balances would have been if Arlen Company had revenue of $300,000 but had received $302,000 cash from customers. These transactions are entered in the following accounts:

Cash		Accounts Receivable	
Beg. bal. 7		Beg. bal. 42	From customer 302
From customer 302		Sale 300	
End. bal. 309		End bal. 40	

Revenues	
	Sale 300

The preceding accounts show that, in this situation, the ending balance of Cash would have been $2,000 larger than the Cash balance when cash receipts equaled sales revenues, as shown earlier. The Accounts Receivable balance would have been $2,000 smaller than the balance when cash receipts equaled sales revenues. Revenues in 2006 would still have been $300,000.

This example shows that, if the ending balance in Accounts Receivable were *less* than its beginning balance, the increase in Cash would be *more* than the amount of Revenues. Part of the increase in Cash would be the result of decreasing Accounts Receivable. Put another way, Cash increased partly because more old customers paid their bills and partly because of sales to new customers. This is what happened in Arlen Company.

Because the increase in Cash was more than the amount of Revenues, we must add to net income the amount that Cash was greater than Revenues. This is $2,000, which is the amount entered in Exhibit 9.2.

Current Asset Balance Increases

If Accounts Receivable had increased during the period, the adjustment of net income would be the opposite; that is, an increase in a noncash current asset leads to an adjustment that subtracts from net income in order to find the cash flow from operations.

Analysis with Diagrams

Let's repeat this analysis, this time using diagrams. The situations illustrated are those in which the beginning balance of Accounts Receivable was $100,000 and additions during the year from sales to customers (revenues) were $800,000. The following diagram shows the situation in which the ending balance in Accounts Receivable was the same as the balance at the beginning of the year.

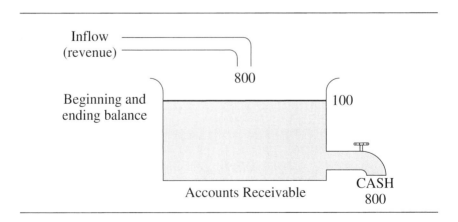

We calculate the inflow to Cash as:

Beginning Balance	$100
Ending Balance	−100
Change	0
Revenue	800
Flow to Cash	800

Thus, if the balance in Accounts Receivable is unchanged, the inflow to Cash is the same amount as revenue and an adjustment is not necessary.

Next consider the situation in which the ending balance in Accounts Receivable was less than the beginning balance, as illustrated in the following diagram:

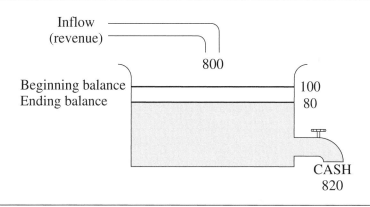

We calculate the inflow to Cash as:

Beginning Balance	$100
Ending Balance	−80
Change	20
Revenue	800
Flow to Cash	820

Thus, if the ending balance in Accounts Receivable is less than the beginning balance, the inflow to Cash is more than the amount of revenue, so we must add to net income in order to show the effect on cash.

Finally, consider the situation in which the ending balance in Accounts Receivable was greater than the beginning balance, as illustrated in the following diagram:

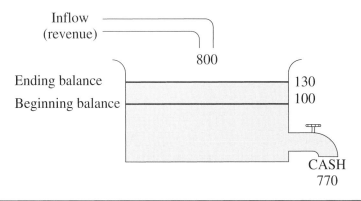

Beginning Balance	$100
Ending Balance	−130
Change	(30)
Revenue	800
Flow to Cash	770

Thus, if the ending balance in Accounts Receivable is greater than the beginning balance, the inflow to Cash is less than the amount of revenue, and we subtract from net income in order to show the effect on Cash.

As shown in Exhibit 9.1, the beginning balance in Inventory was $56,000, and the ending balance was $60,000, which shows that this asset increased by $4,000 during the year. This change had the opposite effect on Cash from the change in Accounts Receivable. Therefore, we must subtract from net income to arrive at the change in cash. The $4,000 subtraction is shown in Exhibit 9.2.

If the balance in a working capital account is unchanged, the inflow to Cash is the same amount as revenue, and an adjustment is not necessary.

To summarize, we must analyze changes in the balance sheet accounts to determine their impact on Cash. We are interested in the working capital accounts to prepare the "Cash Flows from Operating Activities" section of the statement of cash flows.

An easy way to remember whether the impact on Cash (and hence the adjustment to net income) is an addition or a subtraction is to pretend that only that one account and Cash exist. For example, if Cash and Accounts Receivable were the only accounts, a decrease in Accounts Receivable would have to mean an increase in Cash.

This follows from the fundamental accounting equation:

Assets = Liabilities + Equity

To keep this equation in balance, a decrease in Accounts Receivable would necessarily mean an equal increase in Cash, if these were the only two accounts involved. This makes sense because, if everything else remains the same, a decrease in Accounts Receivable means more cash payments to the entity's Cash account.

A change in a current asset may not have an immediate effect on Cash. For example, an increase in Inventory may be accompanied by an increase in Accounts Payable. However, the ultimate effect on Cash for each separate transaction is as described, and the effect from the other accounts will be considered when we analyze those accounts.

ADJUSTMENTS FOR CHANGES IN CURRENT LIABILITIES

Changes in current liabilities have the opposite effect on Cash from changes in current assets. An increase in a current liability requires that the net income amount be adjusted to a cash basis by adding to it. A decrease in a current liability requires that the adjustment be a subtraction.

Exhibit 9.1 shows that Accounts Payable decreased by $3,000. Therefore, net income is adjusted to a cash basis by subtracting this amount.

Exhibit 9.1 shows that Accrued Wages increased by $4,000. Therefore, net income is adjusted to a cash basis by adding this amount to it.

NET EFFECT OF WORKING CAPITAL CHANGES

Using Exhibit 9.2, we can find the net effect of the adjustments on converting net income to a cash basis: There was a net decrease of $1,000. Exhibit 9.2 shows that, although cash increased, the increase in Cash was $1,000 less than net income.

In summary, an increase in current assets means that more of the cash inflow was tied up in Accounts Receivable, Inventory, and/or other current assets, with a corresponding decrease in Cash. This is why, when cash is low, a business tries to keep the other current assets as low as feasible.

Also, an increase in current liabilities means that more cash was freed up. The cash not paid to suppliers is still in the Cash account. This is why, in times when cash is low, a business tries to keep current liabilities as high as feasible.

Users of financial statements need to understand these relationships, but there is no need to memorize them. The cash flow statement gives the net effect of each of the four types of adjustments in working capital items. The following summarizes them:

Change	Adjustment to Net Income
Decrease in a current asset	add
Increase in a current asset	subtract
Decrease in a current liability	subtract
Increase in a current liability	add

Remember that these adjustments are made to convert the net income number to a cash basis. The net income number, as reported on the income statement, is *not changed.*

To complete the "Cash Flow from Operating Activities" section of Exhibit 9.2, we see that cash flow from operating activities was $29,000.

Note that the $6,000 adjustment for Depreciation Expense is larger than the net amount of all the working capital account adjustments. This is the case in some companies, especially manufacturing companies that have relatively large amounts of fixed assets.

As a shortcut, therefore, some analysts arrive at the operating cash flow simply by adding Depreciation Expense to Net Income. They disregard changes in the working capital accounts on the assumption that these changes net out to a minor amount. This shortcut may give the impression that depreciation is a cash flow. Such an impression is erroneous.

Also, since the statement of cash flows is a required financial statement, it is a good idea to read it and obtain the operating cash flow information directly from it.

SUMMARY OF OPERATING ADJUSTMENTS

If the total amount of working capital (excluding cash) did not change, and if there are no noncash expenses, such as depreciation, cash flow from operations will be the same as net income.

If the net amount of the working capital accounts (excluding cash) decreased, cash flow from operations will be higher than net income. Cash was released from working capital accounts.

If the net amount of the working capital accounts (excluding cash) increased, cash flow from operations will be lower than net income. More cash was tied up in working capital accounts.

If there was depreciation expense, cash flow from operations will be higher than net income.

When analyzing the impact on cash from changes in working capital accounts, we must be careful to exclude the cash account from this calculation.

CASH FLOW FROM INVESTING AND FINANCING ACTIVITIES

Exhibit 9.2 shows that, in addition to cash flow from operating activities, there are two other categories on a statement of cash flows: cash flow from investing activities and cash flow from financing activities.

Investing Activities

When a company invests in additional property or plant, the amount involved is a cash outflow from the company. The amount may not be an immediate net decrease in cash because the payment of cash may have been offset by borrowing an equal amount. Nevertheless, it is recorded as a cash outflow, and the amount of the borrowing is recorded separately as a *financing activity*.

As shown in Exhibit 9.1, Arlen Company had Plant at the beginning of 2006 that had cost $108,000. It had $120,000 of Plant at the end of 2006. As shown in Exhibit 9.2, the increase of $12,000 was an investing activity in 2006. (The parentheses indicate that this was a cash outflow.)

The amount of new plant acquired may have been more than $12,000—say, $15,000; the difference of $3,000 would represent cash obtained from the sale of existing plant. Both transactions are investing activities. However, we cannot obtain a breakdown of the amount from the available information. Organizations often provide this breakdown on the statement of cash flows or elsewhere in the notes to their financial statements.

Similarly, if the Plant account decreased, representing the sale of plant assets, there would have been an inflow of cash.

An investing activity is not always a cash outflow.

Financing Activities

Companies may obtain cash by issuing debt securities, such as bonds. Issuing debt securities is a financing activity.

As shown in Exhibit 9.2, Arlen Company had a liability, mortgage bonds. The amount was $34,000 at the beginning of 2006 and $40,000 at the end of 2006. The increase of $6,000 showed that Arlen Company issued bonds of this amount. This was a financing activity. It represented an increase in cash, as shown in Exhibit 9.2.

Similar to the transaction discussed earlier, the amount of new bonds issued may have been more than $6,000. Part of the new issue may have been used to pay off existing bonds. The issuance and redemption of bonds are financing activities.

The borrowings reported in the financing section are both short-term and long-term borrowings. While short-term borrowings often appear as current liabilities, changes in them are reported in the section "Cash Flow from Financing Activities." For example, the current portion of long-term debt is a current liability. For the purpose of cash flow analysis, it is reported as a financing activity.

For example, the current portion of long-term debt is a current liability. For the purpose of cash flow analysis, it is reported as a financing activity.

Issuance of additional shares of a company's stock is also a financing activity. Exhibit 9.1 shows that Arlen Company's Paid-in Capital was $60,000 at the beginning of 2006 and $60,000 at the end of 2006. Evidently, the company did not issue additional stock in 2006.

Dividends paid are classified as a financing activity. Exhibit 9.1 shows that Arlen Company paid $10,000 of dividends in 2006. This amount is shown in Exhibit 9.2.

Generally accepted account principles (GAAP) classify other types of cash flows as either investing or financing. The investing category includes both making investments and disposition of investments; for example, sale of an item of plant is classified as an investing activity, as is the acquisition of an item of plant. Similarly, the financing category includes the repayment of borrowings, as well as cash received from loans. Because the statement of cash flows shows how each item is classified, users do not need to memorize these GAAP rules.

A financing activity is not always a cash inflow.

COMPLETING THE STATEMENT OF CASH FLOWS

We next calculate the increase in cash by summing the three categories in Exhibit 9.2. Note that the $13,000 net increase in cash equals the change in the cash balance as reported on the two balance sheets in Exhibit 9.1.

The cash flow statement shows that, although net income was $24,000 in 2006, Cash increased by only $13,000. Operating activities generated $29,000 in cash; $10,000 of this cash was used to pay dividends. The remaining additional cash inflow was used to acquire new Plant. The cost of the new assets was $12,000; $6,000 of this cost was financed by additional borrowing, and cash was used for the remainder. From the cash inflows, $13,000 remained in the Cash account.

USES OF THE STATEMENT OF CASH FLOWS

A forecast of cash flows helps management and other users of financial information to estimate future needs for cash. For example, when a company is growing, the increase in its accounts receivable, inventory, and fixed assets may require more cash. Therefore, although growth may result in additional profits, it may generate the need for additional cash.

When a company is in financial difficulty, it may pay more attention to its cash flow statement than to its income statement. It pays bills with cash—not net income. Lenders want to know if cash flows are adequate to pay interest on debt and to repay the principal when it becomes due. Analysts generally want to know how much of the annual cash flows come from *sustainable operating activities.* Similarly, shareholders want to know about the adequacy of cash flow to pay dividends.

A number that is useful for these purposes is called **free cash flow.** It is calculated by subtracting from the cash flow expected from operating activities (1) the cash needed to purchase normal fixed asset replacements, (2) the cash required to pay long-term debt that is coming due, and (3) normal dividend payments. The difference indicates the amount, if any, that the company is likely to have available (1) to provide a cushion against unforeseen cash outflows and (2) to provide for other spending that it might like to undertake.

KEY POINTS TO REMEMBER

- A required financial statement, the statement of cash flows, reports the changes in balance sheet accounts as positive or negative impacts on cash during the accounting period.

- The statement has three sections: "cash flow from operating activities," "cash flow from investing activities," and "cash flow from financing activities."

- The cash flow from operating activities is found by adjusting net income for (1) depreciation expense and (2) changes in noncash current assets and current liabilities.

- Depreciation expense is not a cash flow. Because it decreases net income, it is added back to net income in order to arrive at the cash flow from operating activities.

- In general, investing activities include the acquisition of new fixed assets and the proceeds of selling fixed assets.

- In general, financing activities include obtaining funds from long-term borrowing, repaying these borrowings, and obtaining funds from issuance of additional stock.

- GAAP has specific requirements for determining which cash flows are classified as investing activities and which are classified as financing activities, but statement users need not memorize these rules because they are evident from the statement itself.

- When a company is growing or when it is experiencing financial crisis, it may pay more attention to the statement of cash flows than to the income statement. Cash flows from sustainable operating activities are often a focus for analysts.

PART 10

Analysis of Financial Statements

This part describes
- The limitations of financial statement analysis
- The nature and limitations of auditing
- An approach to analyzing financial statements
- Overall financial measures of performance
- Other ratios used in financial statement analysis
- How to detect high vs. low quality earnings
- The basics of the Sarbanes-Oxley Act of 2002

LIMITATIONS OF FINANCIAL STATEMENT ANALYSIS

In this part, we describe how information in financial statements is *used.* Before doing this, we review the reasons that accounting cannot provide a complete picture of the status or performance of an entity.

First, one limitation is suggested by the word "financial"; that is, financial statements report only events that can be measured in monetary amounts.

Second, financial statements are historical; that is, they report only events that *have* happened, while we are also interested in estimating events that *will* happen. The fact that an entity earned $1 million last year is not necessarily an indication of what it will earn next year.

Third, the balance sheet does not show the fair value of nonmonetary assets. In accordance with the asset-measurement concept, plant assets are reported at their unexpired cost. Also, depreciation is a write-off of cost. It is *not* an indication of changes in the real value of plant assets. The balance sheet does not show the entity's "net worth."

Fourth, the accountant and management have some latitude in choosing alternative ways of recording an event in the accounts. An example of flexibility in accounting is that, in determining inventory values and cost of sales, the entity may use the LIFO, FIFO, or average-cost method. Such choices impact the company's net income.

Fifth, many accounting amounts are estimates. In calculating the depreciation expense of a plant asset, for example, one must estimate its service life and residual value.

AUDITING

All large companies and many small ones have their accounting records examined by independent certified public accountants. This process is called **auditing,** and the independent accountants are called auditors.

After completing their examination, the auditors write a report, giving their opinion. This opinion is reproduced in the company's annual report. A typical opinion is shown in Exhibit 10.1.

Note that the opinion says that the auditors *audited* the financial statements and that these statements are the responsibility of management. The opinion further states that the financial statements *fairly present* the financial results. In the last paragraph of the opinion, the auditors assure the reader that the statements were prepared in conformity with generally accepted accounting principles. Note that, since we are referring to Garsden Company's 2004 and 2005 financial statements, the report will not appear until early 2006.

Exhibit 10.1 is an example of a *clean,* or *unqualified,* opinion. If any of the statements cannot be made, the auditors call attention to the exceptions in what is called a *qualified* opinion. A qualified opinion can be a serious matter. If the qualification is significant, securities exchanges can suspend trading in the company's stock.

OVERALL FINANCIAL MEASURES OF PERFORMANCE

Although they have limitations, financial statements usually are the most useful source of information about an entity. We shall focus first on what they tell about its overall *performance.*

Exhibit 10.1

REPORT OF INDEPENDENT AUDITORS

The Board of Directors and Shareholders
Garsden Company

We have audited the accompanying balance sheets of Garsden Company as of December 31, 2006 and 2005, and the related statements of income and cash flows for each of the three years in the period ended December 31, 2006. These financial statements are the responsibility of the company's management. Our responsibility is to express an opinion on these financial statements based on our audits.

We conducted our audits in accordance with generally accepted auditing standards. Those standards require that we plan and perform the audit to obtain reasonable assurance about whether the financial statements are free of material misstatement. An audit includes examining, on a test basis, evidence supporting the amounts and disclosures in the financial statements. An audit also includes assessing the accounting principles used and significant estimates made by management, as well as evaluating the overall financial statement presentation. We believe that our audits provide a reasonable basis for our opinion.

In our opinion, the financial statements referred to above present fairly, in all material respects, the financial position of Garsden Company at December 31, 2006 and 2005, and the results of its operations and its cash flows for each of the three years in the period ended December 31, 2006, in conformity with generally accepted accounting principles.

Archibald and Lake

Seattle, Washington
21 February 2007

Equity investors (i.e., shareholders) invest money in a business in order to earn a profit, or **return**, on that equity (ROE). Thus, from the viewpoint of the shareholders, the best overall measure of the entity's performance is the return that was earned *on* the entity's equity.

The accounting name for the profit or return earned in a year is net income. Return on equity is the percentage obtained by dividing net income by equity.

Example. In 2006, Arlen Company had a net income of $24,000, and its equity on December 31, 2006, was $130,000. Its ROE for 2006 was

$$\frac{\text{Net income}}{\text{Equity}} = \frac{\$24,000}{\$130,000} = 18.5\% \text{ ROE}$$

In order to judge how well Arlen Company performed, its 18.5% ROE must be compared with something. If, in 2005, Arlen Company had an ROE of 20%, we can say that its performance in 2006 was worse than in 2005. This is the **historical** basis of comparison.

If, in 2006, another company had an ROE of 15%, Arlen's ROE was better than the other company's. Or if, in 2006, the average ROE of companies in the same industry as Arlen was 15%, Arlen's ROE was better than the industry average. This is the **external** basis of comparison. If the other company is thought to be the best-managed company in the industry, this comparison is called **benchmarking.**

Finally, if, from our experience, we *judge* that a company such as Arlen should have earned an ROE of 20% in 2006, we conclude that Arlen's ROE was worse than this **judgmental standard.**

Most comparisons are made in one or more of the following three ways:

1. Historical: comparing the entity with its own performance in the past
2. External: comparing the entity with another entity's performance or industry average
3. Judgmental: comparing the entity with a standard based on our judgment

Arlen Company's net income in 2006 was $24,000. Baker Company's net income in the same year was $50,000. From this information we cannot tell which company performed better because we do not know Baker Company's equity. If Baker Company's equity was $1,000,000 and its net income was $50,000, then its ROE would be 5% ($50,000/$1,000,000). With an ROE of 18.5%, Arlen Company performed better than Baker Company.

The comparison of Arlen Company's dollar amount of net income with Baker's dollar amount did not provide useful information. The comparison of their ratios or percentages was useful. Useful comparisons involve ratios or percentages.

FACTORS AFFECTING RETURN ON EQUITY

Ratios help explain the factors that influenced return on equity. Some ratios were explained in earlier parts. We shall review these ratios and introduce others, using the financial statements of Arlen Company in Exhibit 10.2.

Exhibit 10.2

ARLEN COMPANY

Factors Affecting Return on Equity
(Year 2006, $000 Omitted)

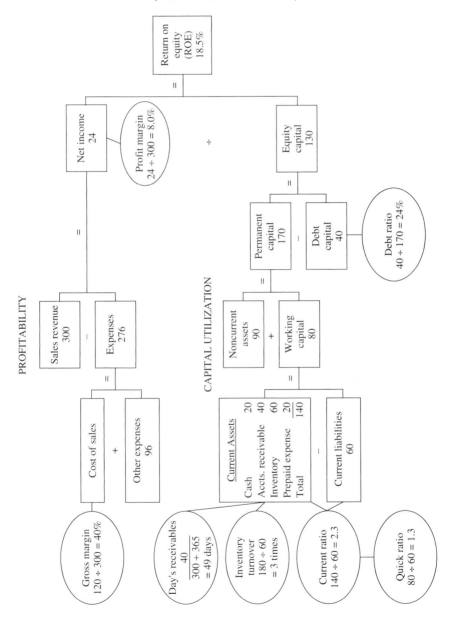

Exhibit 10.3

SOME COMMON RATIOS

Overall Performance	Numerator	Denominator
1. Return on equity (ROE)	net income	equity
2. Earnings per share	net income	number of shares of common stock outstanding
3. Price-earnings ratio	average market price	earnings per share
4. Return on permanent capital	EBIT*	permanent capital**
Profitability		
5. Gross margin %	gross margin	sales revenue
6. Profit margin %	net income	sales revenue
7. EBIT margin %	EBIT*	sales revenue
Capital Utilization		
8. Day's sales uncollected	accounts receivable	sales revenue ÷ 365
9. Inventory turnover	cost of sales	inventory
10. Current ratio	current assets	current liabilities
11. Quick ratio	current assets – inventory	current liabilities
12. Debt ratio	noncurrent liabilities	noncurrent liabilities + equity
13. Capital turnover	sales revenue	permanent capital**

* EBIT means Earnings before Interest and Taxes.

** Permanent capital = noncurrent liabilities + equity.

These ratios are summarized in Exhibit 10.3. We have already described the Return on Equity ratio.

One factor that affects net income is gross margin. In an earlier part, we calculated the **gross margin percentage.** For Arlen Company, this is

$$\frac{\text{Gross margin}}{\text{Sales revenue}} = \frac{\$120}{\$300} = 40\% \text{ gross margin percentage}$$

(From here on, when calculating these ratios, we will omit the three zeros to reduce pencil work; that is, we write 120 instead of 120,000.)

Gross margin percentages vary widely. A profitable supermarket may have a gross margin of only 15%. Many manufacturing companies can have gross margins of about 35%. Compared with these numbers, the gross margin of Arlen Company is high. Since companies even in the same industry can differ widely, it is often misleading to generalize about financial statistics.

A high gross margin does not necessarily lead to a high net income. Net income is what remains after expenses have been deducted from the gross margin, and, the higher the expenses, the lower the net income.

The **profit margin percentage** is a useful number for analyzing net income. We calculated it in an earlier part. We now calculate it for Arlen Company:

$$\frac{\text{Net income}}{\text{Sales revenue}} = \frac{\$24}{\$300} = 8\% \text{ profit margin}$$

Statistics on the average profit margin percentage in various industries are published and can be used by Arlen Company as a basis for comparison. Statistics on the average *dollar* amount of net income are not published. Such statistics are not useful because sheer size is not a good indication of profitability.

TESTS OF CAPITAL UTILIZATION

The bottom section of Exhibit 10.2 shows the main components of Arlen Company's capital. The information is taken from its balance sheet. We shall describe ratios that are useful in understanding these components.

As background for this analysis, let's examine some relationships in Camden Company, which has the following condensed balance sheet:

Assets		Liabilities and Equity	
		Total liabilities....................	$ 400,000
		Total equity	600,000
Total	$1,000,000	Total	$1,000,000

If net income was $60,000, Camden Company's return on equity (ROE) was Net income ÷ Equity, or 10%. If Camden Company could reduce its equity to $500,000, while still maintaining its net income of

$60,000, its ROE would become 12%. Thus, with net income held constant, Camden Company can increase its ROE by decreasing its equity.

Since total assets always equal liabilities plus equity, equity can be decreased only if (1) assets are decreased, (2) liabilities are increased, or (3) there is a combination of these two types of changes.

> ***Example.*** Equity would be decreased by $100,000 (to $500,000) if assets were decreased by $40,000 (to $960,000) and liabilities were increased by $60,000 (to $460,000). If equity were $500,000 and net income were $60,000, ROE would be
>
> $$\frac{\$60,000}{\$500,000} = 12\%$$

Thus, in examining how well an entity used its capital, we need to ask two questions:

1. Were assets kept reasonably low?
2. Were liabilities kept reasonably high?

Let's start with the current assets. If current assets are reasonably low in relation to sales volume, this has a favorable effect on ROE.

In earlier parts, two ratios for measuring current assets were described. One related to accounts receivable and was called the **days' sales uncollected.** It shows how many days of sales revenue are tied up in accounts receivable.

Days' sales uncollected for Arlen Company are

$$\frac{\text{Accounts receivable}}{\text{Sales revenue} \div 365} = \frac{\$40}{\$300 \div 365} = 49 \text{ days}$$

The amount of capital tied up in inventory can be examined by calculating the **inventory turnover ratio.** Since inventory is recorded at cost, this ratio is calculated in relation to cost of sales, rather than to sales revenue.

We can calculate the inventory turnover ratio for Arlen Company as

$$\frac{\text{Cost of sales}}{\text{Inventory}} = \frac{\$180}{\$60} = 3 \text{ times}$$

If Arlen Company had maintained an inventory of $90,000 to support $180,000 cost of sales, its inventory turnover would have been two times, rather than three times. With this change, its ROE would have been lower than the 18.5% shown in Exhibit 10.2.

The **current ratio** is another way of examining the current section of the balance sheet. In an earlier part, we pointed out that, if the ratio of current assets to current liabilities is too low, the company might not be able to pay its bills. However, if the current ratio is too high, the company is not taking advantage of the opportunity to finance current assets with current liabilities. Additional current liabilities would increase its ROE. Equity inevitably would be lower; otherwise, the balance sheet would not balance.

The current ratio for Arlen Company is

$$\frac{\text{Current assets}}{\text{Current liabilities}} = \frac{\$140}{\$60} = 2.3$$

If Arlen Company decreased its current ratio to 1.5 by increasing its current liabilities, this would increase its ROE. However, such a low current ratio would increase the possibility that Arlen would be unable to pay its current liabilities when they come due.

The numbers used here to calculate the current ratio are amounts as of the end of the year. Seasonal factors may greatly affect the current ratio during the year. For example, a department store may increase its inventory in the fall in anticipation of holiday business, and its current ratio therefore decreases. Similar limitations affect the other measures discussed in this part.

A variation of the current ratio is the **quick ratio** (also called the acid-test ratio). In this ratio, inventory is excluded from the current assets, and the remainder is divided by current liabilities. This is a more stringent measure of immediate bill-paying ability than the current ratio. The quick ratio for Arlen Company is

$$\frac{\text{Current assets} - \text{Inventory}}{\text{Current liabilities}} = \frac{\$140 - \$60}{\$60} = 1.3 \text{ times}$$

The final ratio we shall use in examining capitalization is the **debt ratio.** As explained in Part 8, this is the ratio of debt capital to total permanent capital. Noncurrent liabilities are debt capital, and noncurrent liabilities plus equity is total permanent capital. The debt ratio for Arlen Company is

$$\frac{\text{Noncurrent liabilities}}{\text{Noncurrent liabilities} + \text{Equity}} = \frac{\$40}{\$40 + \$130} = 24\%$$

The larger the proportion of permanent capital that is obtained from debt, the smaller the amount of equity capital that is needed. If Arlen had obtained $85,000 of its $170,000 permanent capital from debt, its debt ratio would have been 50%, and its ROE would have been higher than the 18.5% shown in Exhibit 10.2. However, as we learned in Part 8, a high debt ratio results in a more risky capital structure than does a low debt ratio.

In several of the preceding calculations, we used balance sheet amounts taken from the ending balance sheet. For some purposes, it is more informative to use an *average* of beginning and ending balance sheet amounts. Arlen Company had $130,000 of equity at the end of 2006. If it had $116,000 at the beginning of 2006, its *average* equity during 2006 was $123,000. Since its net income in 2006 was $24,000, its return on *average* equity investment was 19.5%.

OTHER MEASURES OF PERFORMANCE

Another measure of performance is **earnings per share.** As the name suggests, the ratio is simply the total earnings (or net income) for a given period, divided by the number of shares of common stock outstanding.

Exhibit 9.1 shows that the earnings (i.e., net income) of Arlen Company in 2006 were $24,000 and that the number of shares outstanding during 2006 was 4,800. Therefore, earnings per share was $5.

Earnings per share is used in calculating another ratio—the **price-earnings ratio.** It is obtained by dividing the average market price of the stock by the earnings per share. If the average market price for Arlen Company stock during 2006 was $35, then the price-earnings ratio is the ratio of $35 to $5, or 7 to 1. Price-earnings ratios of many companies are published daily in the financial pages of newspapers. Often, the ratio is roughly 9 to 1, but it varies greatly, depending on market conditions. If investors think that earnings per share will increase, this ratio could be much higher—perhaps 15 to 1. Apparently, investors are willing to pay more per dollar of earnings in a growing company.

We have focused on return on equity (ROE) as an overall measure of performance. Another useful measure is the **return on permanent capital.** This shows how well the entity used its capital, without considering how much of its permanent capital came from each of the two sources: debt and equity. This ratio is also called **return on investment (ROI).**

The *return* portion of this ratio is *not* net income. Net income includes a deduction for interest expense, but interest expense is the return on debt capital. Therefore, net income understates the return earned on all permanent capital. Also, income tax expense often is disregarded, so as to focus on pretax income.

The return used in this calculation is *earnings before the deduction of interest and taxes on income.* It is abbreviated by the first letters of the words, or **EBIT.**

As with other income statement numbers, earnings before interest and taxes (EBIT) is expressed as the percentage of sales revenue. This gives the EBIT margin. For Arlen Company, this comes to

$$\frac{\text{EBIT}}{\text{Sales revenue}} = \frac{\$42}{\$300} = 14\% \text{ EBIT margin}$$

The permanent capital as of December 31, 2006, is the debt capital (i.e., noncurrent liabilities) of $40,000 plus the equity capital of $130,000, a total of $170,000. The return on permanent capital is found by dividing EBIT by this total:

$$\frac{\text{EBIT}}{\text{Permanent capital}} = \frac{\$42}{\$170} = 25\%$$

Another ratio shows how much sales revenue was generated by each dollar of permanent capital. This ratio is called the **capital turnover ratio:**

$$\text{Capital turnover} = \frac{\text{Sales revenue}}{\text{Permanent capital}} = \frac{\$300}{\$170} = 1.8 \text{ times}$$

American manufacturing companies have a capital turnover ratio of roughly two times on average. A company that has a large capital investment in relation to its sales revenue is called a **capital-intensive** company. A capital-intensive company, such as a steel manufacturing company or a public utility, has a relatively low capital turnover.

Another way of finding the return on permanent capital is to multiply the EBIT margin ratio by the capital turnover. This relationship can be shown as

$$\text{EBIT margin} \times \text{Capital turnover} = \text{Return on permanent capital}$$
$$14\% \qquad \times \qquad 1.8 \qquad = \qquad 25\%$$

This formula suggests two fundamental ways in which the profitability of a business can be improved:

1. Increase the EBIT margin.
2. Increase the capital turnover.

Exhibit 10.3 summarizes the ratios discussed in this part.

PROFITABILITY MEASUREMENT

In the preceding analysis, we used ratios because absolute dollar amounts are rarely useful in understanding what has happened in a business. Also, we focused on *both* income and the capital used in earning that income. Focusing on just one of these elements can be misleading.

For example, consider the following results for a supermarket and a department store, each with $10 million of sales revenue.

	Supermarket	Department store
	($000 omitted)	
Sales revenue	$10,000	$10,000
EBIT	400	2,000
Permanent capital	1,000	5,000

The EBIT margin for the supermarket is only 400/10,000 = 4%, while, for the department store, it is 2,000/10,000 = 20%.

However, the department store has more expensive fixtures, a larger inventory, and a lower inventory turnover than the supermarket, so its capital turnover is lower:

	Sales	÷ Permanent Capital	= Capital turnover
Supermarket	$10,000	÷ $1,000	= 10 times
Department store	$10,000	÷ $5,000	= 2 times

The return on permanent capital is the same in both companies, as we can see from the following calculation:

	EBIT margin	× Capital turnover	= Return on permanent capital
Supermarket	0.04	× 10 times	= 40%
Department store	0.20	× 2 times	= 40%

TESTS OF FINANCIAL CONDITION

A business must be concerned with more than profitability. It must also maintain a sound financial condition. This means that it must be able to pay its debts when they come due.

Ability to meet current obligations is called **liquidity.** The ratio of current assets to current liabilities, called the current ratio, is a widely used measure of liquidity.

Solvency measures the entity's ability to meet all its obligations when they come due. If a high proportion of permanent capital is obtained from debt, rather than from equity, this increases the danger of insolvency. The proportion of debt is indicated by the debt ratio.

Any dozens of other ratios can be used for various purposes in analyzing the profitability and financial condition of business. Those described here are the ones in most general use. Others give a more detailed picture of the important relationships. Financial analysts form their opinions about a company partly by studying ratios such as those presented in this part. They also study the details of the financial statements, including the notes that accompany these statements. They obtain additional information by conversations and visits because they realize that the financial statements tell only part of the story about the company.

QUALITY OF EARNINGS

Quality of Earnings is a term used most often by investors or analysts interested in evaluating a stock, a set of securities or even just the financial statements of a company. It involves analysis that goes beyond the ratio analysis introduced earlier in this chapter.

Information found in the financial statements has limitations. Sometimes investors want to dig deeper to evaluate the **quality** of a company's net income (earnings) or other reported financial data. A quality of earnings analysis typically allows an analyst to evaluate performance in a more comprehensive way than simple ratio analysis.

Typically, ratio analysis involves the use of accounting data as reported. Since accountants have choices when preparing financial statements, the data presented could look different if different choices had been made. To evaluate the quality of a company's earnings, analysts often make adjustments to the reported numbers. This does not mean that the reported numbers are incorrect!

Golden Company's net income might be exactly the same as Silver Company's net income. Golden Company's revenues and expenses might all come from regular and recurring business activities. Silver Company's revenues might come partially from a one-time event not expected to happen again in the future. An analyst would likely say that Golden Company's earnings are a higher quality than Silver Company's earnings.

Evergreen Company turns its revenues into cash inflows within 30 days on a regular basis. River Company allows it customers to buy on credit and they typically don't collect these accounts receivable for many months. The current ratios of both companies might be identical. Investors are likely to say that River Company's current assets are of a lower quality than Evergreen's.

Analysts and investors use indicators other than the performance ratios described earlier to evaluate the quality of a company's reported earnings. Not all analysts define quality of earnings in the same way. Therefore a quality of earnings analysis is a very subjective process.

You have learned that not all revenues are received in cash at the time of a sale. You have also learned that not all expenses are paid out in cash at the time they are incurred. Therefore, net income is not necessarily a good indicator of cash earnings.

Investors often equate "real earnings" with those that generate **cash** from year to year. For these investors real earnings may be more important than net income when determining profitability.

You have learned that the statement of cash flows indicates cash flow from operating activities, from investing activities and from financing activities. Investors think of **real earnings** as normal, recurring operating activities that generate cash. Obviously the statement of cash flows is an extremely useful part of financial statement analysis.

Since investors and analysts look for different things in their analyses, there are no commonly agreed-upon standards for a quality of earnings analysis. Some of the ratios you calculated earlier may be part of a quality of earnings analysis.

Some of the characteristics of companies with high quality of earnings* are:

A. Consistent and conservative accounting policies
B. Net income (earnings) from recurring rather than one-time events
C. Sales revenues that result in cash inflows sooner rather than later
D. Debt that is appropriate for the business, capital structure and industry
E. Earnings that are stable, predictable, and indicative of future earnings levels.

---

*Much of this material is from Leslie Pearlman (Breitner), "Quality of Earnings," © Harvard Business School, 1988.

Most of these issues are beyond the introductory nature of this book. We will explore them in a simple manner to illustrate the concept of **earnings quality.** Some of the work that investors and analysts used to do to determine the quality of a company's earnings has been diminished with the passage of the Sarbanes-Oxley Act (SOX) of 2002. We will explore SOX later in this chapter.

The exhibits below indicate potential quality of earnings in different situations:

A. Consistent and conservative accounting policies (because LIFO and accelerated depreciation result in lower earnings):

	High-Quality Earnings	Low-Quality Earnings
FIFO and straight-line depreciation		X
LIFO and accelerated depreciation	X	

B. Net income (earnings) from recurring activities (because net income is not indicative of future earnings and is not predictable):

	High-Quality Earnings	Low-Quality Earnings
Earnings from activities other than the company's basic business activity		X
Earnings from the ongoing fundamental business of the company	X	

C. Sales resulting in timely cash inflows (because earnings that are not potentially distributable in cash are not what most investors seek):

	High-Quality Earnings	Low-Quality Earnings
Revenues received in cash at the time (or near) of sale	X	
Revenues that stay in Accounts Receivable for long periods of time		X

D. Appropriate debt and capital structure levels (because higher debt may mean it will be more difficult to obtain additional debt financing in the future or the interest rate will likely be higher than the present debt):

	High-Quality Earnings	Low-Quality Earnings
Increasing levels of debt relative to equity		X
Debt levels consistent with the industry and ability of the company to meet its obligations	X	

E. Stable and predictable earnings (because investors want to be more certain of future earnings rather than to anticipate surprises):

	High-Quality Earnings	Low-Quality Earnings
Current and recent earnings that are good indicators of future earnings streams	X	
Current and recent earnings that fluctuate, are from foreign operations, or are from extraordinary events		X

You learned that financial statements tell only a part of the story of a company. **Red flags** or warnings about a company's financial condition that might not show in a typical ratio analysis might be detected in a quality of earnings analysis. Warning signals are often identified early in the analysis to help direct the focus of the analysis. Thus, one reason for thinking about a company's quality of earnings is to detect red flags. While detecting red flags is useful for investors and analysts, this process is very subjective. It is usually the beginning of a more detailed analysis.

Quality-related red flags should not be ignored. They may suggest potential problems not indicated by a more typical ratio analysis. This means that investors and analysts must understand fully the accounting practices as well as the nature and behavior of financial statement items to be able to detect red flags.

Below are some typical quality-related **red flags** and the appropriate financial statement to look at to detect these warning signals.

	Balance Sheet	Income Statement	Both	Neither
A. An unusually long audit report or one that indicates a change in auditors (because the audit report covers all three financial statements – the balance sheet, the income statement and the statement of cash flows – and might indicate disagreement between the auditor and management)				X
B. An increase in Accounts Receivable not consistent with the past (because the company might encourage sales by allowing customers more time to pay)	X			
C. A one-time source of income (because the company might be encouraged to sell an asset to increase its profits)		X		
D. An increase in borrowing (because the company might be having problems financing its activities from internally-generated funds)	X			
E. A slowdown of the inventory turnover rate (because sales, inventory or production problems might be developing)			X	

THE SARBANES-OXLEY ACT OF 2002

Most of us heard about the collapse of Enron Corporation and related accounting scandals. However, even experienced financial analysts were unable to forecast these events through an examination of the financial statements of companies like Enron. The American Competitive and Corporate Accountability Act of 2002, commonly known as the Sarbanes-Oxley Act (SOX), was passed into law in the wake of corporate financial scandals. Its primary purpose was to strengthen corporate governance and rebuild trust in the corporate sector.

Sarbanes-Oxley is a law passed in 2002 to strengthen corporate governance and restore investor confidence. The law is complex. It specifies corporate responsibilities and criminal penalties for noncompliance with the standards. Company management and boards of directors must now be familiar with the details of SOX.

The Sarbanes-Oxley Act was an enormous change to federal securities laws in the United States. It came in response to the collapse of Enron (and other companies) and the related accounting scandal by Enron's auditors, Arthur Andersen. Public companies are now required to submit annual reports on their internal accounting controls to the Securities and Exchange Commission (SEC). Evidently, company management and boards of directors must now be familiar with the details of the Sarbanes-Oxley Act (SOX).

All companies should be concerned about **governance** (authority and control). Since SOX generally affects only publicly-traded companies, it is about corporate governance. SOX affects U.S. companies as well as foreign companies operating in the United States.

The Sarbanes-Oxley Act is detailed and technical. Most issues related to **compliance** are well beyond the introductory nature of this book. However, there are some general areas related to SOX that we will examine. Since SOX is **law** it is critical that companies know how to conform or make their operations compliant.

The costs of noncompliance may be great. They may include both civil and criminal penalties. Since managers concerned with **internal** operations are not generally experts in SOX compliance, they often hire external consultants to help identify areas of potential noncompliance. Evidently those who are experts in SOX must understand both the accounting issues and the legal ones.

Simply put, Sarbanes-Oxley addresses the following:

- Establishment of a Public Company Accounting Oversight Board (PCAOB) under the SEC to oversee public accounting firms and issue accounting standards

- New standards for corporate boards of directors

- New standards for accountability and criminal penalties for corporate management

- New independence standards for external auditors

With new standards and rules set by the PCAOB we can be confident of more detailed annual reports from public companies. Such reports will include a focus on internal controls and ethical behaviors for financial officers. One can hope that SOX will help to increase public confidence.

"Whistle blowers" are those who have publicly exposed undesirable or unlawful behavior by companies. This term comes from the notion that blowing a whistle calls attention to something. SOX also provides extended whistle blower protection to employees who disclose private information about their employers as long as those disclosures are within the law.

SOX has also made it a crime to destroy or conceal documents that might be used in official proceedings. Presumably company officials will now be discouraged from such behavior. Because such tampering is a criminal activity, penalties and jail may be the result. While nonprofit organizations are currently not required to adhere to the majority of SOX regulations, they must comply with regulations related to document destruction and whistle blower protection. Many nonprofit organizations are starting to implement policies that follow the spirit of SOX.

In summary, SOX has provided the oversight and structure to encourage annual reports that are more comprehensive and detailed. In so doing the new law requires the behavior and disclosure on the part of management to increase public confidence and trust.

KEY POINTS TO REMEMBER

- The financial statements do not tell the whole story about an entity because they report only past events, do not report market values, and are based on judgments and estimates. Nevertheless, they provide important information.

- Financial statements are analyzed by using ratios, rather than absolute dollar amounts. These ratios are compared with those for the same entity in the past, with those for similar entities, and with standards based on judgment.

- An overall measure of performance is return on equity (ROE). It takes into account both profitability and the capital used in generating profits. Another overall measure is return on permanent capital, or return on investment, which is the ratio of profits (adjusted for interest and taxes) to total permanent capital.

- An entity with a low profit margin can provide a good return on equity investment if it has a sufficiently high capital turnover.

- In addition to information about profitability, financial statements provide information about the entity's liquidity and solvency.

- Quality of earnings analysis helps investors and analysts to identify "red flags" or warnings. This type of analysis is often used to determine the riskiness of stocks. It goes beyond a simpler and more usual customary financial performance analysis.

- The Sarbanes-Oxley Act of 2002 (SOX) is complex and detailed. In essence it is a law designed to increase disclosure of all material events that could affect financial reporting. Further, it defines unethical and unlawful behavior that could give rise to criminal and civil penalties.

PART 11

Nonprofit Financial Statements

This part describes
*   The nature of nonprofit organizations
*   How financial statements of nonprofit organizations are different
*   How equity differs from net assets
*   Why ratio analysis for nonprofits may be different from their for-profit counterparts

NONPROFIT ORGANIZATIONS

In earlier parts, you learned that, when revenues are greater than expenses, the result of such **profitable** operations is net income or profit. You learned also that the equity section of the balance sheet reports the amount of capital that the entity has obtained from its shareholders or owners, as well as the income that has been retained in the account called Retained Earnings.

Some entities have no **ownership.** Such entities do not obtain capital from shareholders and do not pay dividends. These entities are called **nonprofit,** or **not-for profit,** organizations. For our purposes, both of these terms have the same meaning.

Some examples of organizations with no ownership are museums, hospitals, colleges and universities, private schools, research organizations, churches and synagogues, cultural organizations, foundations, social service organizations, and advocacy groups. Although these organizations may be very different from each other, they all share one trait. They do not have shareholders or owners.

Nonprofit organizations are exempt from paying taxes in most states. The regulations to determine nonprofit status may differ from state to state. To qualify as a nonprofit organization, application must be made to the governing body in the state in which the organization resides.

In Part 2, you learned that the terms "profit," "earnings," "surplus," and "income" all have the same meaning. They refer to the *excess* of revenues less expenses. Nonprofit organizations can have the equivalent of profitable operations, however. To simplify, for nonprofit entities, we often just use the term **surplus,** or excess of revenues less expenses.

Remember that the Equity section of the balance sheet reports the amount of **capital** that the for-profit entity has obtained from two different sources:

1. The amount paid in by the owner(s), which is called paid-in capital
2. The amount of income that has been retained in the entity, which is called retained earnings

Since no dividends are paid in nonprofit organizations, the retained earnings are equal to the **accumulated surpluses.** Some nonprofit organizations do receive **contributions** from persons outside the entity. They are not called **paid-in capital** but are indeed sources of capital.

Nonprofit entities also have three basic financial statements. The status report for a nonprofit is similar to the balance sheet and is called a **statement of financial position.** The flow report is similar to the income statement and is called a **statement of activities.** The third statement, called a **statement of cash flows,** has the same name in a nonprofit entity.

Just like the balance sheet, the statement of financial position reports amounts for the organization's assets, liabilities, and equivalent of equity. Since there is no equity or ownership in a nonprofit, this last term is the **net difference** between the assets and the liabilities and is called **net assets.**

In a for-profit entity, the operating **expenses** (or activities) portrayed on the income statement cause equity to increase or decrease. Similarly, in a nonprofit, the change in net assets is reflected in its statement of activities, the equivalent of the income statement. Finally, a nonprofit reports the change in its **cash** and cash equivalents in a statement of cash flows.

MISSIONS AND GOALS

A primary goal of a for-profit enterprise is to earn a profit. Therefore, the financial statement that measures this best is the income statement. You learned earlier that a good analysis must incorporate information from all three financial statements. This is because all of the financial statements together provide information on different aspects of **financial performance.**

Nonprofit organizations are very different from for-profits with respect to their purpose, or **mission.** If we seek to **measure their performance** using only the monetary amounts, we would neglect important aspects of their missions and goals. Therefore, the financial statements limit the information we have for **measuring performance** to those aspects that can be expressed in monetary amounts.

Some of a nonprofit's goals can be measured using financial statement information. For nonprofits, however, the surplus is not always an appropriate measure. **Performance measures** need to be tied to goals and therefore are likely to be different for nonprofit organizations.

Tools like the Balanced Scorecard have been developed to help focus on many more perspectives related to a company's performance than the financial perspective.

NET ASSETS

One important difference in a balance sheet or statement of financial position of a nonprofit is the term "Net Assets." This term represents the portion of the statement that is occupied by equity in a for-profit organization. Net Assets are classified based on the existence or absence of donor-imposed restrictions.

Three types of net assets must be reported on a statement of financial position. The types are distinguished from one another based on the level of **restriction** imposed on them by donors. The three types are

1. **Permanently restricted** net assets
2. **Temporarily restricted** net assets
3. **Unrestricted** net assets

Some assets are **donated** so that they are maintained permanently by an institution rather than used up. Usually the donors allow the institution to use income generated from investing these assets. While the income can support general operating activities, the assets themselves cannot be spent. Such assets fit into the category of **permanently restricted net assets.**

Sometimes assets are donated for **specific uses,** in a designated accounting period. Once used for the special purpose for which they were intended, they are no longer available. Thus, for the temporary period when they are not being used, the organization may invest them. These assets are called **temporarily restricted assets.**

Unrestricted net assets are those that result from profitable operating activities or from donations with no restrictions.

There are many examples of assets in each of the three categories. If a donor gave land to an organization to use as part of ongoing operations, this donation would fit into the category of permanently restricted net assets. This is because the *purpose of the donation* would be for the permanent future operations of the organization. Likewise, the donation of works of art to a museum would be considered permanently restricted net assets.

The donation of funds for a specific program to take place in May 2007, however, would fit into the category of temporarily restricted net assets. This is because the funds would be used up after the program ended. Until May 2007, however, the funds could not be used for other purposes.

If you receive a phone call from someone asking you to donate funds to your college and you agree to do so, those funds would *likely* fit into the category of unrestricted net assets. Unless you specify that your donation is to be saved for a *specific purpose,* or saved indefinitely and invested for a monetary return, they would show on the statement of financial position in the category *unrestricted net assets.* The classification of net assets is thus either restricted or unrestricted, depending on the intentions of the donor.

It is important to understand the intentions of donors as they affect how organizations can subsequently use funds. There are more complications with respect to the classification of net assets that go beyond the scope of this book.

REVENUES, EXPENSES, AND INVESTMENTS

Revenues are realized for nonprofits in much the same way as they are in for-profit organizations. Remember the **realization concept,** which states that revenue is recognized when goods and services are delivered, so, when a nonprofit organization provides services, it recognizes the revenue associated with this service.

The distinction between a revenue and an inflow of cash is treated much the same way as it is in a for-profit entity. If services are provided in 2006 but are not paid until 2007, the revenue is recognized in 2006 in keeping with the realization concept. When this happens, the account called Accounts Receivable is debited in 2006, with the accompanying credit to sales revenue.

Revenues from **contributions** are different from revenues earned on services provided. Recall that all revenues ultimately increase net assets (similar to their role in increasing equity in a for-profit). In a nonprofit, revenues are considered increases in unrestricted net assets unless the use of the assets received is limited. Similarly, **expenses** are considered decreases in unrestricted net assets.

If a donor imposes a restriction on a contribution, the revenue from that contribution will ultimately increase temporarily restricted net assets or permanently restricted net assets. Since revenues from services provided and revenues from contributions can both be considered unrestricted, both types of revenues will appear together on a statement of unrestricted activities.

The classification of revenues and expenses within the three categories of net assets does not preclude the organization from incorporating additional classifications or explanations within a statement of activities. For example, within a category of net assets, the nonprofit organization may distinguish between **operating** and **nonoperating** items.

Some contributions do not qualify as revenues. For example, contributions of works of art, historical treasures, and similar assets need not be recognized as revenues if the donated items are added to collections held for public exhibition, education, or research to further public service rather than financial gain.

Apparently, the accounting for many transactions for nonprofit organizations is more complex than for-profit accounting.

Some nonprofits have **funds invested** in a way that will provide dividend, interest, or noncash returns. According to accounting regulations for nonprofit organizations, the **gains** and **losses** on such investments must be reported as increases or decreases in unrestricted net assets unless their use is temporarily or permanently restricted by the donor or by the law. This means that, in addition to revenues from operating activities and from contributions, revenues from investments will also appear as increases in unrestricted net assets. This can make the interpretation of the financial statements of a nonprofit very challenging.

The investment portion of an organization's assets derived from donations is called an **endowment.** An endowment can earn a **return** for the organization in several different ways. For example, funds invested in bonds or put into a bank earn **interest.** Interest income is a source of revenue. Unless the use of interest earned is restricted, it will be reported as revenue in the statement of unrestricted activities.

Funds can also be invested in stocks of private entities. Recall from earlier parts that some companies pay **dividends** to shareholders. Although a nonprofit organization does not have shareholders (or stockholders) or owners, it can own stock in another company as an investment. Dividends earned from stock investments will also be reported as revenues in the statement of unrestricted activities, according to accounting regulations.

Investments may be made in stocks that don't pay dividends or in bonds that don't pay interest. Investors hope that such investments will result in higher stock or bond prices at some time in the future.

Sometimes, the organization does not sell stocks or bonds that have increased in value but decides to hold them for the future. At the end of each accounting period, the organization must determine the **market value** of these investments, too. Although the gain, if there is one, is not realized unless the stock is sold, it must be reported as revenue. This **unrealized gain** is just as much a part of revenues on the statement of unrestricted activities as dividends and interest or other realized gains.

Exhibit 11.1

Mercer Community Services
Statements of Financial Position
($000 Omitted)

Assets

	As of June 30	
	2006	2005
Assets:		
Cash and cash equivalents.....................................	$ 38	$ 230
Accounts receivable	1,065	835
Inventories...	200	350
Prepaid Expenses	105	150
Contributions receivable	1,512	1,350
Land, buildings, and equipment...........................	33,313	33,725
Long-term investments	109,035	101,750
Total assets..	$145,268	$138,390

Liabilities and Net Assets

Liabilities and Net Assets:		
Accounts payable..	$ 1,285	$ 525
Refundable advances		325
Grants payable	438	650
Notes payable...		570
Long-term debt	2,750	3,250
Total liabilities	4,473	5,320
Net assets:		
Unrestricted...	57,614	51,835
Temporarily restricted.......................................	12,171	12,735
Permanently restricted	71,010	68,500
Total net assets	140,795	133,070
Total liabilities and net assets	$145,268	$138,390

Mercer Community Services
Statements of Activities
($000 Omitted)
Year Ended June 30, 2006

	Unrestricted	Temporarily Restricted	Permanently Restricted	Total
Revenue, gains, and other support:				
Contributions...................................	$4,320	$4,055	$140	$8,515
Fees..	2,700			2,700
Income on long-term investments....	2,800	1,290	60	4,150
Other investment income..................	425			425
Net realized and unrealized				
gains on long-term investments......	4,114	1,476	2,310	7,900
Other..	75			75
Net assets released from restrictions:				
Satisfaction of program restrictions	5,995	(5,995)		
Expiration of time restrictions........	1,375	(1,375)		
Total revenue, gains, and other support	21,804	(549)	2,510	23,765
Expenses and losses:				
Program X...	6,550			
Program Y	4,270			
Program Z	2,880			
Administration	1,250			
Fundraising.......................................	1,075			
Other losses......................................		15		30
Total expenses	16,025	15		16,040
Change in net assets:...........................	5,779	(564)	2,510	7,725
Net assets at beginning of year.............	51,835	12,735	68,500	133,070
Net assets at end of year	57,614	12,171	71,010	140,795

The financial statements for Mercer Community Services in Exhibit 11.1 are typical of those for a nonprofit organization. Mercer had investments that provided income, realized gains, and unrealized gains.

Also, there were restrictions on some of the investment income. The income on Mercer's long-term investments fit into all three categories (unrestricted, temporarily restricted, and permanently restricted). Mercer had both unrealized and realized gains on its long-term investments. In Exhibit 11.1, the total net realized and unrealized gains on all categories of long-term investments were $7,900,000.

The total amount of revenue that Mercer received from fees from its services was $2,700,000. This was 12.4% of the total unrestricted revenues for the period ending June 30, 2006. Unrestricted revenues from contributions amounted to 19.8% of the total unrestricted revenues for the period ending June 30, 2006.

If the financial statements for Mercer Community Services are typical for nonprofits like Mercer, it is customary that fees from services make up the majority of unrestricted revenues.

TRANSFERS

As you learned earlier, sometimes contributions from donors are recorded in the category of temporarily restricted. This means that there is a designated *purpose* for the contribution specified by the donor. Funds must remain in the temporarily restricted category of net assets until the accounting period when they are used for the designated purpose. As restricted funds are used for their designated purpose, they must be transferred from their holding pattern to the unrestricted category on the statement of activities. This transfer of funds allows the reader to see that the entity has used funds held for a specific purpose.

Current operating activities of a nonprofit entity are found in the unrestricted revenues and expenses on the statement of activities. Therefore, contributions for activities that are to take place in the future will not be recorded in the unrestricted portion of the statement of activities. Rather, they will stay in the category of temporarily restricted net assets until such time as they are used.

Although the total amount of net assets will not change as a result of a transfer, the individual categories will change. The sum total of all transfers is zero. To be certain you understand how the transfer process works, recall the closing process from Part 3. In Part 3, you learned that income statement accounts are temporary accounts and balance sheet accounts are permanent accounts. This will help you to understand how transfers work.

You also learned that, ultimately, revenues increase the equivalent of equity and that expenses decrease the equivalent of equity. This, too, will help you to understand how transfers work. If a nonprofit organization, for example, received a contribution of $5,000 in 2006 for a program to take place in 2007, the journal entry would be

```
Dr. Cash (temporarily restricted) ..$5,000
    Cr. Revenues
    (temporarily restricted).......    $5,000
```

The journal entry to close the temporarily restricted revenue account to net assets at the end of 2006 would be

```
Dr. Revenues
(temporarily restricted) ...........$5,000
   Cr. Net Assets
   (temporarily restricted) .......    $5,000
```

In 2007 when the program takes place, the journal entry would be

```
Dr. Net Assets
(temporarily restricted) ...........$5,000
   Cr. Revenues (unrestricted) .....    $5,000
```

At the end of 2007, the unrestricted revenues account will close to unrestricted net assets. In Exhibit 11.1, you can see the amount of the transfer from temporarily restricted net assets to unrestricted net assets. The total amount of transfers is $7,370 and the net effect of the transfers is zero. Use the exhibit to see that revenues for the period 2006 increase net assets and expenses decrease net assets. The beginning amount of unrestricted net assets for 2006 is $51,835. The total of unrestricted revenues for 2006 is $21,804, and the total of unrestricted expenses is $16,025. The surplus, or change in net assets, is $5,779. If you add the beginning net to the change in net assets, you arrive at the ending unrestricted net assets figure of $57,614.

SIMILARITIES TO FINANCIAL STATEMENTS OF FOR-PROFIT ENTITIES

The financial statements of nonprofit organizations are similar to those of for-profit companies in almost as many ways as they are different. For example, nonprofit organizations are required to recognize the cost of using up long-lived tangible assets. However, depreciation need not be recognized for certain works of art and historical treasures.

Nonprofit organizations must prepare a statement of cash flows to accompany the statement of financial position and the statement of activities. This statement of cash flows looks very much like the ones you learned about in Part 9.

LIMITATIONS OF RATIO ANALYSIS

In Part 10, you learned to use some tools to measure financial performance. Equity investors invest in a business to earn a profit. Nonprofit organizations do not have equity investors, so the return on equity is somewhat meaningless for these entities. This does not mean that we should ignore the surplus, or the difference between revenues and expenses.

You also learned about the amount of capital tied up in inventory by looking at the inventory turnover ratio. Many nonprofit organizations do not use inventory in the way that for-profits use it. Often, the inventory in nonprofits is a supplies inventory rather than a sales inventory. This makes the inventory turnover ratio potentially meaningless for performance measurement, too.

A ratio is the relationship between the numerator and the denominator. Before measuring performance using a ratio, we must ask if both the numerator and the denominator have meaning for the analysis we are trying to do. If the answer is no, then another type of performance measure may be better.

The financial statements tell only a part of the story about an entity. Since nonprofits have many goals that are nonfinancial, we must develop other measures of performance.

KEY POINTS TO REMEMBER

- Some entities have no ownership; such organizations are nonprofit, or not-for-profit, organizations.

- Nonprofit organizations have three financial statements, just as for-profit businesses have: the statement of financial position, the statement of activities, and the statement of cash flows.

- Net assets is the portion of the statement of financial position occupied by equity on a balance sheet. The three categories of net assets are unrestricted, temporarily restricted, and permanently restricted.

- Revenues from contributions must be classified as unrestricted, temporarily restricted, or permanently restricted. Revenues from services provided are unrestricted revenues.

- Both realized and unrealized gains on investments are reported as unrestricted revenues.

- Transfers from temporarily restricted funds occur when the funds are used for their specified purpose.

- The interpretation of ratios is different in nonprofit organizations than in for-profit organizations. Ratios have meaning only to the extent that both their numerator and denominator are appropriate measurements.

- Nonprofit organizations have many goals that are nonfinancial. Appropriate performance measures must be chosen to complement the information provided in their financial statements.

PART 12

Government Accounting

This part describes
- The nature of government accounting as it differs from private and nonprofit organizations
- The different levels of government and the accounting regulatory bodies associated with them
- The nature of stewardship and accountability in the public sector
- How federal, state, and local government accounting practices are different from one another

THE NATURE OF GOVERNMENT ACCOUNTING

The concepts presented here reflect government accounting in the United States. There may be significant differences when examining the financial reporting practices in other countries. A portion of the material in this section was provided by the Government Accounting Standards Board (GASB).

In Part 11 you learned about financial statements for **nonprofit organizations** and how they differ from those of private companies. This part is about financial statements for **governments.** Financial reporting for government entities is different from both private companies and nonprofit organizations. Accounting for government entities is different from accounting for other entities and is more complicated. One of the reasons that government accounting can be difficult is that, in most cases, there is no single government entity. In this part we will consider some of the differences among U.S. government entities.

Business entities are formed to create **profits** (net income) for their owners or shareholders. Governments exist to serve citizens. They don't have owners or shareholders (or stockholders).

A primary contrast of the relationship between citizens and their government and between shareholders and their business entities is the involuntary nature of the former and the voluntary nature of the latter. In the same way as shareholders invest in businesses as owners, the public "owns" government. But that ownership is involuntary. Because citizens are taxed involuntarily to provide resources, they demand a high degree of **accountability** from government.

The principal purpose of government is to serve its citizens. In general, businesses in the private sector could not make a profit providing the same services. So, governments end up providing the services that are deemed necessary. Government performance is judged on its ability to provide well for its citizens.

Citizens hold governments **accountable** for providing services. Thus a primary role for government financial reporting is to demonstrate accountability. A primary role for business financial reporting is to demonstrate profitability.

Most businesses generate **revenues** from sales or services provided. That is, a customer **exchanges** money for a good or service from a business. Similarly, creditors or lenders exchange money for the right to earn interest on the debt they provide to businesses. In contrast, governments get revenues from nonexchange transactions. In nonexchange transactions governments receive value from citizens without directly giving equal value in exchange or they give value to citizens without receiving equal value.

There are other ways in which government accounting differs from business accounting. One of these is the way assets are treated. Recall from Part 1 that business accounting focuses on the fair value of monetary assets and on the cost of nonmonetary assets. This concept is called the asset-management concept.

Remember too that assets must be owned or controlled by the entity, they must be **valuable,** and they must be acquired at a measurable cost. In general, being a valuable asset for a business means that it will generate future cash flows. The future benefit for government is the ability of the asset to provide services and goods that are the mission of the government.

The permanent nature of most governments also affects government accounting. Although business accounting is based on the going-concern concept (it assumes the entity will continue to operate indefinitely) the focus is still on the ability of assets to produce revenues and on the fair value of assets and liabilities. For governments, the focus is on the ability to **provide and sustain services.** Rather than profitability, government financial reporting focuses on sustainability.

LEVELS OF GOVERNMENT

There are different financial reporting standards for federal, state, and local governments. Just as there are regulations for the **financial statements** of private and nonprofit entities, federal government agencies, state agencies, and local governments (counties, cities, and towns) must prepare financial statements.

Part of the complexity in government accounting is due to the different agencies that set the reporting standards. In the United States, the Financial Accounting Standards Board (FASB) regulates the accounting practices for private and nonprofit entities. The Government Accounting Standards Board (GASB) is the regulatory agency for state and local government accounting.

Understanding **federal financial accounting** is the most complex of the three areas (private, nonprofit, government). One reason for this is the size of the federal government and its multi-purpose nature. There is a separate **F**ederal **A**ccounting **S**tandards **A**dvisory **B**oard that establishes accounting principles for federal entities. The FASAB must work together with the FASB and the GASB to coordinate reporting requirements that affect entities that have relationships between them.

The FASAB must consider the information needs of many parties in developing federal accounting standards. The federal government is **accountable** to the public who have an interest or **stake** in its performance. Although there are no owners or shareholders of the government, there are many stakeholders. We can see why accounting and reporting standards are necessary for public accountability.

Often there are interrelationships between and among entities across the private, nonprofit, and government sectors. Obviously what affects entities in one sector can also affect entities in other sectors.

These days many organizations **partner** with those in a different sector to provide services. Such public-private partnerships complicate the need for accurate and timely financial reporting. Likewise, the regulatory agencies also have to partner with each other to coordinate accounting regulations for their entities. For example, the U.S. Department of the Treasury must coordinate with the U.S. Office of Management and Budget (OMB) to prepare and submit the Financial Report of the U.S. government.

To summarize, the three primary regulatory agencies and the types of entities for which they develop financial accounting standards are:

Regulatory Agency	Type of Entity
FASB	Private and Nonprofit
GASB	State and Local Government
FASAB	Federal Government

Users of federal financial information need information to help them assess how well the government is doing in such areas as **budgetary integrity, operating performance, stewardship, and systems control.** These four objectives help to ensure the accountability of the federal government.

Similarly, users of state and local government financial reports seek information about **budgetary compliance, cost and sustainability of services, and adequacy of resources.** These objectives also help state and local governments to demonstrate accountability. Although somewhat different in nature, both the FASAB and the GASB have similar financial reporting objectives.

The U.S. government's principal financial report is the President's annual budget. Hence, the Budget of the U.S. Government is the reference point for taxes as sources of revenues as well as the authority to spend money. **Budgetary integrity** is a key aspect of government accountability. For businesses, the **budget** is an internal working plan or blueprint for the future. For government, the budget is a legal document indicating how resources must be used. The budget authorizes the government to collect revenues and use them to provide services to its citizens.

ACCOUNTABILITY AND PERFORMANCE

Demonstrating accountability for budgetary compliance is a distinguishing objective of government financial reporting. The budget is the instrument to authorize the use of government resources. Because citizens involuntarily provide resources (revenues) to government in the form of taxes, showing budgetary compliance helps to demonstrate accountability.

Just as a Statement of Cash Flows focuses on the sources and use of cash in a particular accounting period, government financial reporting focuses on the sources and uses of budgetary resources and whether they were in accordance with law. That is, government reporting information should inform whether money was spent as intended. This is different from financial reporting for private sector businesses.

Government reporting must also be concerned with whether budgetary resources are sufficient to cover related obligations. The information in government financial reports has both financial and nonfinancial components. Like private companies, government entities must also prepare operating statements and balance sheets based partially on accrual accounting. Accrual-based measures of operating performance may differ from budgetary information for many reasons. Apparently users of government reporting information should understand both the budget as well as the **related** financial statements. To complicate matters more, users must also understand how the two are related to each other.

Measurement of **operating performance** is complex for government entities. Government services are usually not **matched** with or provided in direct exchange for fees. Thus, it is difficult to apply the matching concept as we would in business accounting to arrive at net income, or in nonprofit accounting to arrive at surplus, as **indicators of financial performance.** Further, the change in net assets, as in a nonprofit organization, is not the only indicator of performance. Other nonfinancial indicators of performance, linked to a government's mission, goals, and objectives, should be part of its financial reports.

The measurement of expenses, however, can be matched with services provided. Thus, the actual cost of specific programs and services can be reported and used for a variety of purposes, including the construction of future budgets and the determination of financing needs. Cost of services can also be tracked for purposes of budgetary compliance and comparison to other programs and services. For this reason, government financial reports focus on the details of programs and their associated costs.

Users will want to know whether resources (or revenues) are sufficient to cover the costs of **activities,** both in the current period and in the future. Hence, government financial reports contain a statement of activities, detailed by function and program. The very simple financial statements for Evergreen City, are typical of those of many larger U.S. cities (see Exhibit 12.1).

The management of **assets** and **liabilities** is also a focus of operating performance for a government entity. Typically, these are the items that appear on a balance sheet. When evaluating government performance, readers of the financial statements will want to determine how assets were financed and how they were used. They might also want to know whether the level of debt used to finance assets or provide services has grown over a period of time.

Accounting for assets like property, plant, and equipment is different in government accounting. Recall that businesses use depreciation to turn the acquisition cost of an asset into an expense over a specified period of time. Governments acquire assets in large part to support the services they provide for an indefinite period of time. Further, governments are committed to preserve and maintain assets. Government cost reporting reflects this.

Exhibit 12.1

Evergreen City Statement of Net Assets
($ Millions) 31 December 2006

ASSETS:	Governmental Activities	Business-Type Activities	TOTAL
Non-Capital Assets	$ 15,000	$ 8,000	$ 23,000
Capital Assets, Net of			
Accumulated Depreciation	$ 65,000	$ 52,000	$ 117,000
TOTAL ASSETS	**$ 80,000**	**$ 60,000**	**$ 140,000**
LIABILITIES:			
Current Liabilities	$ 5,000	$ 3,000	$ 8,000
Long-term liabilities	$ 25,000	$ 28,000	$ 53,000
TOTAL LIABILITIES	**$ 30,000**	**$ 31,000**	**$ 61,000**
NET ASSETS:			
Investments in Capital Assets	$ 45,000	$ 26,000	$ 71,000
Net of Related Debt			
Restricted	$ 2,000	$ 1,000	$ 3,000
Unrestricted	$ 3,000	$ 2,000	$ 5,000
TOTAL NET ASSETS	**$ 50,000**	**$ 29,000**	**$ 79,000**

Part of a government's accountability for managing resources is to provide services economically and efficiently and to attain its goals effectively. Hence federal financial reporting focuses on the use of resources in program operations rather than solely on the financial value of those resources.

Stewardship means to take responsibility for resources or to protect and use the resources well. A focus on **stewardship** as reflected in financial reporting is unique to the public sector. Users of government financial reports are interested in whether the government's financial position improved or worsened over the accounting period. Financial statement items that might help in this determination are the balance sheet items assets, liabilities, and net assets. For example, a user might look at the growth of liabilities, or debt over time rather than just the absolute amount of the obligations. The notion of stewardship involves being responsible for more than just the reporting of numbers.

Part of good stewardship is knowing whether the revenues or resources of an accounting period were sufficient to pay for the services of that period. If revenues from prior periods or future periods have to pay for services of the current period, there is lack of **interperiod equity.** Interperiod equity and intergenerational equity are often used to mean the same thing. So, concerns of good stewardship often necessitate the use of nonfinancial as well as financial information. Such concerns are also related to the notion of who pays and who benefits.

Accrual-based measures are the starting point for analyzing **government performance** but we cannot use them alone. While financial reporting typically focuses on historical performance, government financial reports must also have a more forward-looking focus. This differentiates government financial reporting from the private and nonprofit financial statements that we looked at earlier.

In government accounting financial accountability is demonstrated by using both a "current financial resource flows" measurement as well as a "modified accrual basis" of accounting. **Fund reporting** helps to achieve a meaningful relationship between the two. Exhibits 12.1 to 12.6 shows examples of fund accounting in a municipality as well as the statements used to reconcile it with the accrual-based statements.

Another area of focus for government financial reporting is financial management **systems** and internal accounting **controls.** Among other things, such systems and controls should help to prevent fraud, waste, and abuse of government assets. This focus on systems and controls is especially of concern in federal financial reporting. Users of government financial reports should be aware of the primary objectives described above. These objectives make government financial reporting much more complex than reporting for private companies. They are:

> **Budgetary Integrity**
> **Operating Performance**
> **Stewardship**
> **Systems and Controls**

FINANCIAL REPORTING – A MUNICIPALITY

Exhibits 12.1 to 12.6 portray the two levels of financial statements for a municipality that are required by the GASB. Government-wide financial statements (Exhibits 12.1 and 12.4) use accrual-based accounting. Traditional fund accounting statements, prepared using a modified accrual basis of accounting, are also presented here (Exhibits 12.2 and 12.5). The introductory nature of this book permits only a superficial examination of these financial statements. They are included here to illustrate the complex nature of government accounting.

Changes in the reporting requirements for government accounting have determined the way government entities prepare their **financial statements.** To make accounting reports of government entities more useful, accrual accounting is now used. However, traditional fund accounting is also used. This focuses on the flow of financial resources. There are two methods or levels of accounting reflected in the financial statements of government entities.

Exhibit 12.2

Evergreen City Statement of Activities
Year Ended 31 December 2006

| | | Program and Other Revenue | Net (Expenses) Revenue and Changes in Net Assets | | |
| | | | Governmental Activities | Business-Type Activities | TOTAL |
Functions/Programs	Expenses				
Government Activities	$ 15,000	$ 1,000	$ (14,000)		$ (14,000)
Business-Type Activities	$ 5,800	$ 6,000		$ 200	$ 200
TOTAL GOVERNMENT	**$ 20,800**	**$ 7,000**	**$ (14,000)**	**$ 200**	**$ 13,800**
General Revenues:					
Property taxes			$ 13,600		$ (13,600)
Licenses, Permits, Investment income			$ 600	$ 100	$ 700
Change in Net Assets			$ 200	$ 300	$ 500
Beginning Net Assets			$ 49,800	$ 28,700	$ 78,500
Ending Net Assets			**$ 50,000**	**$ 29,000**	**$ 79,000**

Exhibit 12.3

Evergreen City Balance Sheet—Governmental Funds
($ Millions) 31 December 2006

	General	Special Revenue	Capital Projects	Debt Service	Total Governmental Funds
ASSETS:					
Financial	$ 9,000	$ 1,000	$ 3,000	$ 1,000	$ 14,000
Other	1,000	$		$	1,000
TOTAL ASSETS	**$ 10,000**	**$ 1,000**	**$ 3,000**	**$ 1,000**	**$ 15,000**
LIABILITIES:					
Current Liabilities	$ 3,200	$ 800	$	$ 200	$ 4,200
Other	$ 800	$	$	$ –	$ 800
TOTAL LIABILITIES	**$ 4,000**	**$ 800**	**$ –**	**$ 200**	**$ 5,000**
FUND BALANCES:					
Reserved		$ 200	$ 3,000	$ 800	$ 4,000
Unreserved	$ 6,000				$ 6,000
TOTAL FUND BALANCES	**$ 6,000**	**$ 200**	**$ 3,000**	**$ 800**	**$ 10,000**
TOTAL LIABILITIES AND FUND BALANCES	**$ 10,000**	**$ 1,000**	**$ 3,000**	**$ 1,000**	**$ 15,000**

171

Exhibit 12.4

Evergreen City—Governmental Funds Statement of Revenue, Expenditure, and Changes in Fund Balances ($ Millions) Year Ended 31 December 2006

	General	Special Revenue	Capital Projects	Debt Service	Totals
Revenue	$ **7,200**	$ **5,000**	$ **2,000**	$ **1,000**	$ **15,200**
Expenditures:					
Non-capital	$ 5,000	$ 4,800		$ 800	$ 10,600
Debt Service					
Capital			$ 4,000		$ 4,000
Total Expenditures	$ **5,000**	$ **4,800**	$ **4,000**	$ **800**	$ **14,600**
Excess (Deficiency) Revenue over Expenditures	$ 2,200	$ 200	$ (2,000)	$ 200	$ **600**
Beginning Fund Balances	$ 3,800	$ –	$ 5,000	$ 600	$ **9,400**
Ending Fund Balances	$ 6,000	$ 200	$ 3,000	$ 800	$ **10,000**

Exhibit 12.5

Evergreen City Reconciliation of Governmental Funds Balance Sheet to Statement of Net Assets ($ Millions) As of 31 December 2006

Fund Balances as reported in governmental funds balance sheet	**$ 10,000**
Capital assets used in governmental activities are not current financial resources and, therefore, are not reported in the fund balance sheet, but are reported in the governmental activities of the statement of net assets.	$ 65,000
Some long-term liabilities (such as bonds payable) are not due and payable in the current accounting period and therefore not reported in the fund financial statement.	$ (25,000)
Net Assets of Governmental Activities	**$ 50,000**

Exhibit 12.6

Evergreen City Reconciliation of Statement of Revenues, Expenditures and Changes in Fund Balances to Statement of Activities ($ Millions) For the Year Ended 31 December 2006

Net change in fund balances – total governmental funds	**$ 600**
Amount by which depreciation expense on general fixed assets in the statement of activities exceeded capital outlay expenditures in general governmental funds	$ (3,000)
Amount by which proceeds from issuance of bonds exceeded repayments in the current period	$ 2,600
Changes in net assets of governmental activities	**$ 200**

The two levels of financial reporting provide greater opportunity to satisfy the needs of different users of government financial statements. Having more than one type of accounting also makes the interpretation of government financial reports much more difficult than the financial reports of businesses.

Exhibit 12.1 portrays a government-wide statement of net assets. Much like the nonprofit balance sheets we looked at earlier in this book,

Exhibit 12.1 has assets, liabilities, and net assets. Additionally, there are two different types of activities represented on the statement of net assets. Governmental activities are distinguished from business-type activities. Business-type activities are typically those that might charge a fee in exchange for services provided. The statement of net assets is constructed using accrual-based accounting.

As we saw earlier, some government activities involve exchange transactions where fees or revenues are received in exchange for services. Other governmental transactions are nonexchange activities where revenues are collected from citizens but are not directly exchanged for services.

Exhibit 12.2 shows the Statement of Activities for Evergreen City. The statement of activities is similar to the income statement for a business entity or operating statement for a nonprofit organization. The two general categories of items we find on an income statement, an operating statement, and on a statement of activities are revenues and expenses.

Exhibit 12.2 also shows two types of activities: governmental activities and business-type activities, similar to the statement of net assets. Since we can see the revenues and expenses for these two sets of programs, users can determine whether revenues were sufficient to cover expenses in the accounting period for each set of activities.

For which type of activities were the related revenues sufficient to cover expenses? It is not unusual for business-type activities to have revenues at least equal to expenses. This is because business-type activities often involve exchange transactions. Because the "program and other revenues" associated with government activities are not sufficient to cover the related expenses, we must look for other revenues or resources to cover these expenses. The source of the revenues to cover government activities comes from general revenues (property taxes and licenses, permits, and investment income).

Like the financial statements we looked at earlier in this book, the statement of activities is linked to the statement of net assets. You can see from the exhibit that the total net assets on the statement of net assets for governmental and business-type activities are also shown as the ending net assets on the statement of activities. These amounts are $50,000, $29,000, and $79,000.

Exhibits 12.3 and 12.4 are fund accounting statements. Rather than government-wide financial statements, they focus only on governmental funds. Further, these statements are not prepared on the accrual basis but rather are modified. Hence, government reporting must also prepare additional explanatory material to link the fund accounting financial statements with the accrual-based financial statements.

Recall the difference between expenditures and expenses. Notice that Exhibit 12.2 reports expenses while Exhibit 12.4 focuses on expenditures.

We can certainly see why the financial reports of government entities are so complicated.

To help users of these financial statements **reconcile** the accrual-based statements with those prepared used a modified accrual basis; we must also prepare reconciliation statements. Exhibit 12.5 presents the first reconciliation statement. This statement begins with the number for fund balances as reported in the governmental funds balance sheet. See if you can find this $10,000 on Exhibits 12.1, 12.2, 12.3, or 12.4. On Exhibit 12.3, the governmental funds balance sheet, it is in the "total governmental funds" column.

The reconciliation in Exhibit 12.5 adjusts the $10,000 for items not contained in the fund accounting statements. The purpose of this is to reconcile the total fund balances from Exhibit 12.3 with the total net assets on a government-wide basis from Exhibit 12.1. See if you can find the $50,000 on Exhibit 12.1. It is at the bottom of the column labeled governmental activities. The reconciliation statements correct for those items included in the accrual-based statements but not included in the fund accounting statements. Using two levels of accounting complicates the interpretation of financial information. However, the two levels allow different perspectives to be presented in the financial reports.

Exhibit 12.6 presents the second reconciliation statement. This statement reconciles Exhibit 12.2, which focuses on expenses, with Exhibit 12.4 which focuses on expenditures. Find the $600 on Exhibit 12.4. It is called "excess revenue over expenditure." Now find the $200 on Exhibit 12.2. It is in the column labeled "net (expenses) revenue and changes in net assets in the governmental activities."

The reconciliation statements attempt to relate the fund accounting financial statements to the accrual-based statements to help users make sense of the financial information. Indeed, government financial reporting is complicated. Further analysis of government financial statements is beyond the scope of this book. Full government financial reports contain many sets of explanations and notes to help readers make sense of the statements.

Concluding Note

You now know the essentials of accounting. There is, of course, much more to the subject. However, you now have a basic framework into which you can fit many other transactions when you encounter them. Moreover, notes are added to the financial statements which help explain them and give more detail than the statements themselves. You should always read these notes carefully.

We have used a common set of terms throughout this program. Unfortunately, there is no standard set of terms. Companies can use other terminology. Nonetheless, from your knowledge of the nature of the balance sheet and the income statement, you can usually figure out what is meant by a term that is not used in this program.

Some transactions are governed by specific rules that are not described in this introductory treatment.

ACKNOWLEDGMENTS

Dr. Matthew Israel developed the program for the first edition.
Dr. Philip E. Myer, Boston University, developed the original glossary.
Cameron E. H. Breitner contributed in a significant way to Part 8.
Cory Sbarbaro helped with the Sarbanes-Oxley Act and its relationship to nonprofit organizations.
Wendy Craven and Kerri Tomasso of Prentice Hall and Heather Willison of Carlisle Publishing Services were extremely patient and supportive during the revisions for the 9th Edition.
We appreciate the advice and help of these persons.

Glossary

Note: The definitions here are brief and are intended as an introduction to the meaning of the terms. They do not encompass all the nuances or qualifications. For a more full discussion, the concepts are defined in the text.

A

Accelerated depreciation: A method of depreciation that charges off more of the original cost of a plant asset in the earlier years than in the later years of the asset's service life. Used mainly in calculating taxable income.

Account: A record in which the changes for a balance sheet or income statement item are recorded.

Account payable: The amount that the entity owes to a supplier, not evidenced by a note.

Account receivable: An amount that is owed to the business, usually as a result of the ordinary extension of credit to one of its customers.

Accountability: Demonstrating accountability for budgetary

compliance is a distinguishing objective of government financial reporting.

Accounting income: Income measured according to accounting principles. Contrast with taxable income.

Accounting period: The period of time over which an income statement summarizes the changes in equity. Usually the official period is one year, but income statements are also prepared for a shorter, or interim, period.

Accrual accounting: Accounting for revenues in the period in which they are earned and for expenses in the period in which they are incurred. This is normal accounting practice. Cash accounting, which accounts only for cash receipts and payments, is usually not acceptable.

Accrued expense: Another term for accrued liability. Note that this is a liability account, not an expense account.

Accrued liability: A liability that arises because an expense occurs in a period prior to the related cash payment. Example: accrued wages payable.

Accrued pensions: The amount a company owes its employees for the benefits they accumulated under a pension plan. The liability is measured as the benefits accumulate.

Accumulated depreciation: An account showing the total amount of an asset's depreciation that has been accumulated to date. It is subtracted from the cost of the asset; the difference is the asset's book value.

Additional paid-in capital: The amount paid by investors in excess of the par or stated value of the stock.

Advances from customers: A liability account showing the amount due customers who have paid for goods or services in advance of their delivery. Sometimes called deferred revenue, precollected revenue, or unearned revenue.

Allowance for doubtful accounts: The amount of estimated bad debts that is included in accounts receivable. This amount is subtracted from accounts receivable on the balance sheet.

Amortization: The process of writing off the cost of intangible assets. Sometimes used as a name for expensing the cost of all assets.

Asset: A valuable item that is owned or controlled by the entity and that was acquired at a measurable cost.

Asset-measurement concept: Accounting focuses on the fair value of monetary assets and on the cost of nonmonetary assets.

Auditing: An examination of accounting records by independent, outside public accountants.

Authorized stock: The total number of shares of stock that a corporation is permitted to issue. (The total number actually issued is usually a smaller amount.)

Available for sale: The sum of beginning inventory and purchases during the period.

Average-cost method: Finding cost of sales by taking the average cost per unit of the beginning inventory plus purchases.

B

Bad debt: An account receivable that never will be collected.

Bad debt expense: The estimated amount of bad debts applicable to an accounting period.

Balance: The difference between the totals of the two sides of an account. An account has either a debit balance or a credit balance.

Balance sheet: A financial statement that reports the assets, liabilities, and equity of a company at one point in time. Assets are listed on the left and liabilities and equity on the right.

Benchmarking: Comparing an entity's performance against the performance of the company thought to be the best managed in the industry.

Bond: A written promise to repay money furnished the business, with interest, at some future date, usually more than one year hence.

Book value: The difference between the cost and the accumulated depreciation of a depreciable asset.

C

Calendar year: The year that ends on the last day of the calendar, December 31. The accounting period for many entities is the calendar year, but some use the natural business year.

Capital: In general, the amount of funds supplied to an entity. Also used as the name for paid-in capital in a proprietorship or partnership.

Capital-intensive: Characterizes a company that has a large capital investment in relation to its sales revenue.

Capital lease: An item the entity controls by a lease agreement that extends over almost the whole life of the item. A capital lease is an asset.

Capital stock: A balance sheet account showing the amount that the shareholders contributed in exchange for stock. This plus retained earnings equals equity in a corporation.

Capital turnover: A ratio obtained by dividing annual sales by the amount of permanent capital.

Cash: The name for money, whether in currency or in a bank account.

Cash-basis accounting: An accounting system that does not use the accrual basis; it records only cash receipts and payments. Usually not an acceptable basis for accounting.

Cash flow statement (also, Statement of Cash Flows): A financial statement reporting the sources and uses of cash during an accounting period.

Charge (verb): To debit an account.

Claim: Amount owed to creditors or others who have provided money or have extended credit to a business.

Closing entries: Journal entries that transfer the balances in revenue and expense accounts for a period to retained earnings.

Common stock: Stock whose owners are not entitled to preferential treatment with regard to dividends or to the distribution of assets in the event of liquidation. Its book value is not related to its market value.

Comparisons, bases of: Performance can be compared with past performance, with performance of other entities, or with a judgmental standard.

Concepts: Accounting concepts are presented throughout the book.

Conservatism concept: Recognize increases in equity only when they are reasonably certain; recognize decreases as soon as they are reasonably possible.

Consolidated statements: Financial statements prepared for a whole corporate family as an entity. The family consists of a parent and its subsidiaries.

Contra-asset account: An account whose balance is subtracted from that of the corresponding asset account.

Conversion cost: The labor and overhead costs of converting raw material into finished products.

Cost: A monetary measure of the amount of resources used for some purpose. Product costs and acquisition costs are among those presented in the book.

Cost accounting: The process of identifying and accumulating manufacturing costs and assigning them to goods in the manufacturing process.

Cost of goods sold: Same as cost of sales.

Cost of sales: Cost of the same products whose revenues are included in sales revenue.

Credit (noun): The right-hand side of an account or an amount entered on the right-hand side of an account. Abbreviated as Cr.

Credit (verb): To make an entry on the right-hand side of an account. Rules for debit and credit are summarized in the book.

Creditor: A person who lends money or extends credit to an entity.

Current assets: Cash and assets that are expected to be converted into cash or used up in the near future, usually within one year.

Current liabilities: Obligations that become due within a short period of time, usually one year.

Current ratio: The ratio obtained by dividing the total of the current assets by the total of the current liabilities.

D

Days' sales uncollected: The number of days of sales that are tied up in accounts receivable as of the end of the accounting period. Sales per day is found by dividing annual credit sales by 365, and accounts receivable is divided by sales per days to find the days' receivables.

Debit (noun): The left-hand side of an account or an amount entered on the left-hand side of an account. Abbreviated as Dr.

Debit (verb): To make an entry on the left-hand side of an account. Rules for debit and credit are summarized in the book.

Debt capital: The capital raised by the issuance of debt securities, usually bonds.

Debt ratio: The ratio of debt capital to total permanent capital.

Deduction method: Finding cost of sales by adding the beginning inventory and purchases and subtracting the ending inventory.

Deferred income taxes: The difference between the actual income tax for the period and income tax expense.

Deferred revenue: Revenues received as cash in advance of the time period in which the services are provided. See also Advances from customers.

Depletion: The process of writing off the cost of a wasting asset, such as natural gas, coal, oil, or other minerals.

Depreciable cost: The difference between the cost of a plant asset and its estimated residual value.

Depreciation expense: The portion of the estimated net cost of plant assets (e.g., buildings, equipment) that becomes an expense in a given accounting period.

Depreciation rate: The percentage of the cost of an asset that is an expense each year. In the straight-line method, the rate is 1 divided by the service life.

Derivative: An instrument issued by a financial institution that promises to pay interest, for example, derived from underlying obligations such as mortgages. Some companies obtain funds by issuing such instruments backed by other instruments. Also, any type of transaction whose value depends, at least in part, upon the value of a related asset or liability.

Direct labor or materials: The labor or material that is used directly on a product.

Disposition of plant, gain or loss on: The difference between book value and the amount actually realized from a sale of a plant asset.

Dividend: The funds generated by profitable operations that are distributed to shareholders. Dividends are not an expense.

Double-entry system: A characteristic of accounting in which each transaction recorded causes at least two changes in the accounts.

Dual-aspect concept: The total assets of an entity always are equal to its total liabilities and equity.

E
Earnings: Another term for net income.

Earnings before interest and taxes (EBIT): An amount used in calculating return on permanent capital.

Earnings per share: A ratio obtained by dividing the total earnings for a given period by the number of shares of common stock outstanding.

EBIT margin: Earnings before interest and income taxes as a percentage of sales revenue.

Entity: A business or other organization for which a set of accounts is kept.

Entity concept: Accounts are kept for entities, rather than for the persons who own, operate, or are otherwise associated with those entities.

Entry: The accounting record made for a single transaction.

Equation, fundamental accounting: Assets = Liabilities + Equity.

Equity: Capital supplied by (1) equity investors and (2) the entity's retained earnings. Also, claims against the entity by equity investors.

Equity capital: The capital supplied by owners, who are called equity investors.

Exchange transactions: Occur when a customer exchanges money for a good or service from a business. See also Nonexchange Transactions.

Expenditure: The decrease in an asset or increase in a liability associated with the acquisition of goods or services. Do not confuse with expense, which represents the use of goods and services and which may occur after the expenditure.

Expense: A decrease in equity resulting from operations during an accounting period; that is, resources used up or consumed during an accounting period. Example: wage expense. Concepts discussed in the book include assets that will become expenses and expenses that create liabilities.

Expensing: The process of charging the cost of an asset to expense.

Expired cost: Another name for expense.

External basis of comparison: Comparing an entity's performance with the performance of other entities.

F

Face amount: The total amount of a loan that must be repaid, specified on the face of a bond.

Fair value: The amount for which an asset can be sold in the marketplace.

FASAB: The Federal Accounting Standards Advisory Board establishes accounting principles for federal entities in the United States.

FASB: The Financial Accounting Standards Board regulates the accounting practices for private and nonprofit entities.

FIFO (first-in, first-out) method: Finding cost of sales on the assumption that the oldest goods (those first in) were the first to be sold (first out).

Financial statements: See the three required financial statements: balance sheet, income statement, statement of cash flows.

Fiscal year: See Natural business year.

Fixed assets: Tangible, noncurrent assets.

Free cash flow: The amount remaining after special needs for cash in the coming period is subtracted from the cash flow expected from operating activities.

Fringe benefits: Benefits, principally monetary, beyond wages; owed to an employee because of his or her service to the company.

Fund reporting: The means by which a relationship is established between current financial resource flows and the modified accrual basis of accounting for government entities.

G

Gain (or loss) on disposition of plant: The difference between book value and the amount actually realized from a sale of a plant asset.

GASB: The Government Accounting Standards Board is the regulatory agency for state and local government accounting in the United States.

Going-concern concept: Accounting assumes that an entity will continue to operate indefinitely.

Goods available for sale: The sum of the beginning inventory plus purchases during the period.

Goodwill: An intangible asset; the amount paid in excess of the value of a company's identifiable net assets, representing an amount paid for a favorable location or reputation. Goodwill is an asset only if it was purchased.

Government accounting: The format and processes by which government entities on the federal, state, and local levels construct their financial statements.

Gross margin: The difference between sales revenue and cost of sales.

Gross margin percentage: Gross margin as a percentage of sales revenue.

H
Historic cost concept: See Cost concept.

Historical basis of comparison: Comparing an entity's performance with its own performance in the past.

I
Income: The amount by which equity increased as a result of operations during a period of time.

Income statement: A statement of revenues and expenses, and the difference between them, for an accounting period; a flow report. It explains the changes in equity associated with operations of the period.

Income tax: A tax levied as a percentage of taxable income. See Taxable income.

Intangible asset: An asset that has no physical substance, such as goodwill or the protection provided by an insurance policy.

Interest: The amount paid for the use of money. A loan requires payment of both interest and principal.

Interest expense: The entity's cost of using borrowed funds during an accounting period.

Interest revenue: Revenue earned from permitting someone to use the entity's money. Revenue from the "rental" of money. Often but erroneously called interest income.

Interim statements: Financial statements prepared for a period shorter than one year, such as a month or a quarter.

Intrafamily transactions: Transactions between the corporations in a consolidated family. These transactions are eliminated in preparing consolidated financial statements.

Inventory (noun): Goods being held for sale, and material and partially finished products that will be sold upon completion.

Inventory (verb): To conduct a physical observation and count of inventory.

Inventory turnover: A ratio that shows how many times inventory was totally replaced during the year;

calculated by dividing the average inventory into cost of sales.

Investments: Securities that are held for a relatively long period of time and are purchased for reasons other than the temporary use of excess cash. They are noncurrent assets.

Issued stock: The shares of stock that have been issued. Issued stock less treasury stock equals outstanding stock. Contrast with authorized stock.

J

Journal: A record in which transactions are recorded in chronological order. It shows the accounts to be debited or credited and the amount of each debit and credit. Transactions are posted to the ledger.

Judgmental basis of comparison: Comparing an entity's performance with our personal judgment.

L

Land, life of: Except in rare cases, land retains its usefulness indefinitely.

Lease: An agreement under which the owner of property permits someone else to use it. The owner is the lessor. The user is the lessee.

Ledger: A group of accounts. Entries are posted to the ledger from the journal.

Leverage: The proportion of debt capital to total permanent capital. A company that obtains a high proportion of its permanent capital from debt is said to be highly leveraged.

Liability: The equity or claim of a creditor.

LIFO (last-in, first-out) method: Finding cost of sales on the assumption that the goods most recently purchased (last in) were the first to be sold (first out).

Limitations on financial statement analysis: There are many pieces of information one might want when analyzing an organization. The financial statements do not provide all of it.

Liquidity: An entity's ability to meet its current obligations. Often measured by the current ratio.

Losses: Expenses resulting from assets whose future benefit has expired during a period, for example, from fire or theft, and liabilities occurring in a period, for example, from lawsuits. See also Gain (or loss).

M

Manufacturing company: A company that converts raw materials into finished, salable products and then sells these products. There are accounting practices specifically for inventory in a manufacturing company.

Manufacturing overhead: See Production overhead cost.

Marketable securities: Securities that are expected to be converted into cash within a year; a current asset.

Matching concept: Costs that are associated with the revenues of a period are expenses of that period.

Materiality concept: Disregard trivial matters, but disclose all important matters.

Measurable cost: An item whose amount is known, usually because the item was acquired from an outside party.

Merchandising company: A company that sells goods that it has acquired from other businesses; for example, a retail store or a wholesaler.

Minority interest: The equity of those shareholders in a subsidiary other than the equity of the parent. Reported as an equity item on the consolidated balance sheet.

Monetary assets: Cash and promises by an outside party to pay the entity a specified amount of money.

Money-measurement concept: Accounting records report only facts that can be expressed in monetary amounts. Accounting therefore does not give a complete record of an entity.

Mortgage: A pledge of real estate as security for a loan.

Mortgage payable: The liability for a loan that is secured by a mortgage.

N

Natural business year: A year that ends on the day that activities are at a relatively low level. For some entities, the accounting period is the natural business year, rather than the calendar year. Also called the fiscal year.

Net: The amount remaining after something has been subtracted from a gross amount. Example: accounts receivable, net.

Net assets: In a nonprofit organization, the portion of the balance sheet occupied by equity in a for-profit organization. Alternatively, assets–liabilities. Net assets may be unrestricted, temporarily restricted, or permanently restricted.

Net income: The amount by which total revenues exceed total expenses for an account period; the "bottom line." In a nonprofit organization, the surplus.

Net income percentage: Net income expressed as a percentage of sales revenue.

Net loss: The amount by which total expenses exceed total revenues in an accounting period; negative net income. In a nonprofit organization, the deficit.

Net worth: Another (but misleading) name for equity.

Nonbusiness organizations: Municipalities, hospitals, religious organizations, and other organizations that are not operated for the purpose of earning a profit.

Noncurrent asset: An asset that is expected to be of use to the entity for longer than one year.

Noncurrent liability: A claim that does not fall due within one year. Similar to Debt capital.

Nonexchange transactions: When governments receive value from citizens without directly giving equal value in exchange.

Nonprofit or not-for-profit: An entity with no ownership or shareholders. The regulations to determine nonprofit status vary from state to state.

No-par-value stock: Common stock that does not have a par value. It is recorded at its stated value.

Note: A written promise to pay.

Note payable: A liability evidenced by a written promise to pay.

O

Obsolescence: A loss in the usefulness of an asset because of the development of improved equipment, changes in style, or other causes not related to the physical condition of the asset. It is one cause of depreciation; the other cause is wearing out.

OMB: The Office of Management and Budget works with the U.S. Department of the Treasury to prepare and submit the financial report of the U.S. government.

Opinion or opinion letter: The report in which the auditor gives his or her opinion as to the fairness of the financial statements.

Other post-employment benefits (OPEB): Health care or other fringe benefits, besides pensions, owed to an employee after his or her employment ends.

Outstanding stock: Shares of stock held by investors. Consists of issued stock less treasury stock.

Overhead: See Production overhead cost.

Overhead rate: A rate used to allocate overhead costs to products.

Owners' equity: The claims of owners against the assets of a business. In a corporation, owners' equity consists of capital stock plus retained earnings.

P

Package of accounting reports: See Report package.

Paid-in capital: The amount paid by investors in exchange for stock. The amount in excess of the stock's par or stated value is called additional paid-in capital.

Par value: The specific amount printed on the face of some stock certificates. No longer significant in accounting.

Parent: A corporation that controls one or more other corporations because it owns more than 50 percent of their stock. The controlled corporations are its subsidiaries.

Partnership: An unincorporated business with two or more owners.

Patent: A grant that gives an inventor the exclusive right, for 17 years, to produce and sell an invention.

Percentage: A number obtained by dividing one number by another (which is the base, or 100 percent), and multiplying by 100. Income statement items are often expressed as percentages of sales revenue.

Performance, measures of: Often analyzed using ratios, overall measures of performance can be compared to other organizations or to the same organization over its history.

Period costs: Costs associated with general sales and administrative activities. Contrast with product costs.

Permanent account: An account for a balance sheet item, so called because it is not closed at the end of the accounting period. Contrast with temporary account.

Permanent capital: The sum of noncurrent liabilities and equity.

Permanently restricted net assets: In a nonprofit organization, assets donated for specific purposes which cannot be used in other ways.

Perpetual inventory: A record of the cost of each item in inventory showing the quantity and the cost of receipts, issues, and the amount on hand, updated nearly simultaneously for each day's activity.

Physical inventory: The amount of inventory currently on hand, obtained by making a physical count.

Plant assets: All tangible, noncurrent assets except land.

Posting: The process of transferring transactions from the journal to the ledger.

Precollected revenue: See Advances from customers.

Preferred stock: Stock whose owners have a preferential claim over common stockholders for dividends and for assets in the event of liquidation.

Prepaid expenses: The general name for intangible assets that will become expenses in future periods when the services they represent are used up. Example: prepaid insurance.

Price-earnings ratio: A ratio obtained by dividing the average market price of the stock by the earnings per share.

Principal: The amount that must be repaid on a loan. The total repayment consists of principal plus interest.

Product: Goods or services sold or to be sold. Sometimes refers only to tangible goods.

Product costs: The direct materials, direct labor, and production overhead costs of a product. Contrast with period costs.

Production overhead cost: Product costs other than direct materials and direct labor. Includes, for example, supervision, building maintenance, and power. See also Overhead rate.

Profit: Another name for income or surplus.

Profit and loss statement: Another name for income statement.

Profit margin percentage: Net income divided by sales revenue.

Proprietorship: An unincorporated business with a single owner.

Q

Quality of earnings: Some characteristics include consistent and conservative accounting policies, income from recurring activities, revenues and net income that are stable, predictable, and indicative of future cash flow, and appropriate levels of debt.

R

Ratio: The result of dividing one number by another. See, for example, Current ratio.

Real earnings: Earnings that generate cash from year to year and are part of normal, recurring operating activities.

Realization concept: Revenue is recognized when goods or services are delivered, in an amount that is reasonably certain to be realized.

Reasonably certain: A criterion for deciding on the amount to be entered for an asset or liability account.

Recognition: The act of recording a revenue or expense item as being applicable to a given accounting period. Revenue recognition is governed by the realization concept.

Red flags: Warning signals about a company's financial condition that might give hints about the quality of earnings. See also Quality of Earnings.

Rental revenue: Revenue earned from permitting someone to use a building or other property.

Report, Auditors': See Opinion.

Report package: Consists of a balance sheet for the beginning and end of the accounting period and an income statement for the accounting period.

Residual claim: The claim of equity investors.

Residual value: The amount for which a company expects to be able to sell a plant asset for at the end of its service life.

Retained earnings: The increase in equity that has resulted from the operations of the entity. It is an equity item, not an asset.

Return on equity (ROE): A ratio obtained by dividing net income by the amount of equity.

Return on investment (ROI): Earnings before interest and taxes divided by noncurrent liabilities plus equity. (Some people calculate it in other ways.)

Return on permanent capital: Another name for return on investment.

Revenue: The increase in owners' equity resulting from operations during a period of time, usually from the sale of goods or services.

S

Sales income: Sometimes used to mean sales revenue; a misleading term because income is the difference between sales revenue and expenses.

Sales revenue: Revenue from the delivery of goods or services.

Sarbanes-Oxley Act: 2002 law passed to help ensure compliance with accounting regulations and transparency in financial reporting.

Security: An instrument such as a stock or bond. Securities give the entity that owns them valuable rights from the entity that issued them.

Service: An intangible product. Examples are personal services, rent, and insurance protection.

Service life: The period of time over which an asset is estimated to be of service to the entity.

Service revenue: Revenue from the performance of services.

Shareholder equity: The equity section of a corporation's balance sheet. Also called stockholder equity. See also Equity.

Shareholders: The owners of a corporation. Also referred to as stockholders.

Shrinkages: Goods that have been stolen or spoiled and hence are no longer in inventory.

Sole proprietorship: See Proprietorship.

Solvency: An entity's ability to meet its long-term obligations. Often measured by the debt ratio.

Specific identification method: A way of calculating cost of sales by keeping track of the specific item (e.g., an automobile) sold.

Stated value: The amount at which no-par-value stock is reported on the balance sheet, as voted by the directors.

Statement of activities: In a nonprofit organization, the statement of revenues and expenses, or the statement which describes the change in net assets.

Statement of cash flow (also Cash Flow Statement): A financial statement reporting the sources and uses of cash during an accounting period.

Statement of financial position: Another name for a balance sheet.

Stewardship: The notion of stewardship involves being responsible for more than just the reporting of the financial data.

Stock: See Capital stock, Common stock, Preferred stock.

Stock dividend: A dividend consisting of shares of stock in the corporation.

Stock split: An exchange of the number of shares of stock outstanding for a substantially larger number.

Stockholders: See Shareholders.

Straight-line depreciation: A depreciation method that charges off an equal fraction of the estimated depreciable cost of a plant asset over each year of its service life.

Subsidiary: A corporation that is controlled by another corporation, the parent, which owns more than 50 percent of its stock.

Surplus: In a nonprofit organization, the equivalent of profit, income, or earnings.

T

T-account: The simplest version of an account.

Tangible assets: Assets that can be touched; they have physical substance. Noncurrent tangible assets are often referred to as property, plant, and equipment.

Tax depreciation: The depreciation used in calculating taxable income.

Taxable income: The amount of income subject to income tax, computed according to the rules of the Internal Revenue Service. There can be a difference between taxable income and accounting income due to the treatment of depreciation.

Temporarily restricted net assets:
In a nonprofit organization, assets donated for specific purposes in a designated accounting period.

Temporary account: A revenue or expense account. A temporary account is closed at the end of each accounting period. Contrast with Permanent account.

Trademark: A distinctive name for a manufactured good or a service.

Transaction: An event that is recorded in the accounting records; it always has at least two elements.

Transfer: In a nonprofit organization, as funds are used for their intended purposes they are transferred from temporarily restricted funds to the unrestricted category on the statement of activities.

Treasury stock: Previously issued stock that has been bought back by the corporation.

U

Unearned revenue: See Advances from customers.

Unexpired cost: The cost of assets on hand now that will be consumed in future accounting periods.

Units-of-production method: A depreciation method. A cost per unit of production is calculated, and depreciation expense for a year is found by multiplying this unit cost by the number of units that the asset produced in that year.

Unrealized gain: Gains on invested funds, whether such investments are sold for cash or held for the future by an organization.

Unrestricted activities: In a nonprofit organization, those activities reported on the statement of activities matched with unrestricted revenues.

Unrestricted net assets: In a nonprofit organization, net assets that result from profitable operating activities or from donations with no restrictions.

W

Wasting assets: Natural resources, such as coal, oil, and other minerals. The process of charging wasting assets to expense is called depletion.

Whistle blower: Those who publicly expose undesirable or unlawful behavior by companies to call attention to the objectionable practices.

Working capital: The difference between current assets and current liabilities.

Write down: To reduce the cost of an item, especially inventory, to its market value.

Write-off of bad debt: To remove a bad debt from accounts receivable.